The
Victorian
Christmas

The Victorian Christmas

ANNA SELBY

First published in Great Britain in 2008 by
REMEMBER WHEN PUBLICATIONS
an imprint of
Pen & Sword Books Ltd
47 Church Street
Barnsley
South Yorkshire
S70 2AS

ISBN 978 184468 028 3

A CIP catalogue record for this book is
available from the British Library.

Printed and bound in Thailand
By Kyodo Nation Printing Services Co., Ltd

Pen & Sword Books Ltd incorporates the Imprints of
Pen & Sword Aviation, Pen & Sword Family History, Pen & Sword Maritime,
Pen & Sword Military, Wharncliffe Local History, Pen & Sword Select,
Pen & Sword Military Classics, Leo Cooper, Remember When,
Seaforth Publishing and Frontline Publishing

For a complete list of Pen & Sword titles please contact
PEN & SWORD BOOKS LIMITED
47 Church Street, Barnsley, South Yorkshire, S70 2AS, England
E-mail: enquiries@pen-and-sword.co.uk
Website: www.pen-and-sword.co.uk

Contents

Acknowledgements

I have mercilessly plundered various books written during the period, including Chambers' *A Book of Days* and works by Eliza Acton and Mrs Beeton. I would also like to thank Geoffrey Hindley for his helpful advice, Diana Craig for *A Miscellany of Cooks' Wisdom*, Carlotta Barrow for the loan of her original copy of Mrs Beeton and my husband, Philip Cottam, for his endless support and generosity of spirit – and for discovering his great-great-grandmother's recipe book.

Introduction

Christmas has, by definition, been with us for two millennia. It has not, though, always been the kind of festival we know today. Rather, it has had a complex and paradoxical history. At times, it has been celebrated purely within a religious context; at others it has become so entangled with pagan rituals it could be regarded as Christian virtually in name only and it has even, for several years, been banned altogether.

But there was one period when Christmas reigned supreme, bringing together the religious, the charitable, the merriment, the feasting and the general good cheer. Did the Victorians invent Christmas? Certainly, before them, Christmas had nowhere near the importance they were to give to it and which it has retained to this day. The Victorians made Christmas the time when friends and families drew together around the blazing hearth that, above all, symbolised their Christmas. Here, they would tell stories, exchange presents, sing carols, play charades and feast on the finest food they would eat all year. They would not think only of

themselves, however.

Christmas was also a time of charity for the Victorian family. They were exhorted at church services to give to the poor and this they did in abundance. Their Christmas cards – a Victorian invention – were often adorned with pictures of charitable acts. And, of course, their greatest Christmas Story, Dickens' *A Christmas Carol*, tells how the heart of a miser is softened to make him not only charitable to his clerk, Cratchit and his family, but to turn him into a happy and gregarious celebrant of Christmas.

And, if the Victorians could not be said to have invented Christmas itself, they certainly invented many of its most popular trappings. The Christmas pudding, the Christmas card, the Christmas pantomime, Christmas crackers, most of our famous Christmas carols (along with the earlier traditional ones they embellished and generally improved) and Father Christmas himself in the form we know him today. It was Prince Albert who brought the Christmas tree to England from his native Germany and, after a picture showing the royal family crowding around it in wonder, the Christmas tree became, within a very short time – along with the red-coated Father Christmas and the red-breasted robin – symbolic of the English Christmas. Prince Albert also made gingerbread and other German confectionary an essential part of the English Christmas and he is often regarded as one of the men who invented the Victorian Christmas. The other is, without doubt, Charles Dickens. So, draw up a chair to the roaring fire and let Dickens introduce you in the Victorian idea of Christmas.

Dickens's Christmas

Christmas time! That man must be a misanthrope indeed, in whose breast something like a jovial feeling is not roused – in whose mind some pleasant associations are not wakened – by the recurrence of Christmas. There are people who will tell you that Christmas is not to them what it used to be; that each succeeding Christmas has found some cherished hope, or happy prospect, of the year before, dimmed or passed away; that the present only serves to remind them of reduced circumstances and straitened incomes – of the feasts they once bestowed on hollow friends, and of the cold looks that meet them now, in adversity and misfortune. Never heed such dismal reminiscences. There are few men who have lived long enough in the world, who cannot call up such thoughts any day of the year. Then do not select the merriest of the three hundred and sixty-five for your doleful recollections, but draw your chair nearer the blazing fire – fill the glass and send round the song – and if your room be smaller than it was a dozen years ago, or if your glass be filled with reeking punch, instead of sparkling wine, put a good face on the matter, and empty it off-hand, and fill another, and troll off the old ditty

you used to sing, and thank God it's no worse. Look on the merry faces of your children (if you have any) as they sit round the fire.

Who can be insensible to the outpourings of good feeling, and the honest interchange of affectionate attachment which abound at this season of the year. A Christmas family party! We know nothing in nature more delightful! There seems a magic in the very name of Christmas. Petty jealousies and discords are forgotten; social feelings are awakened, in bosoms to which they have long been strangers; father and son, or brother and sister, who have met and passed with averted gaze, or a look of cold recognition, for months before, proffer and return the cordial embrace, and bury their past animosities in their present happiness. Kindly hearts that have yearned towards each other but have been withheld by false notions of pride and self-dignity, are again reunited, and all is kindness and benevolence! Would that Christmas lasted the whole year through (as it ought) and that the prejudices and passions which deform our better nature were never called into action among those to whom they should ever be strangers!

The Christmas family party that we mean, is not a mere assemblage of relations, got up at a week or two's notice, originating this year, having no family precedent in the last, and not likely to be repeated in the next. No. It is an annual gathering of all the accessible members of the family, young or old, rich or poor; and all the children look forward to it, for two months beforehand, in a fever of anticipation. Formerly, it was held at grandpapa's; but grandpapa getting old, and grandmamma getting old too, and rather infirm, they have given up house-keeping, and domesticated themselves with uncle George; so, the party always takes place at uncle George's house, but grandmamma sends in most of the good things, and grandpapa always WILL toddle down, all the way to Newgate-market, to buy the turkey, which he engages a porter to bring home behind him in triumph, always insisting on the man's being rewarded with a glass of spirits, over and above his hire, to drink 'a merry Christmas and a happy new year' to aunt George. As to grandmamma, she is very secret and mysterious for two or three days beforehand, but not sufficiently so, to prevent rumours getting afloat that she has purchased a beautiful new cap with pink ribbons for each of the servants, together with sundry books, and pen-knives, and pencil-cases, for the younger branches; to say nothing of divers secret additions to the order originally given by aunt George at the pastry-cook's, such as another dozen of mince-pies for the dinner, and a large plum-cake for the children.

On Christmas-eve, grandmamma is always in excellent spirits, and after employing all the children, during the day, in stoning the plums, and all that, insists, regularly every year, on uncle George coming down into the kitchen, taking off his coat, and stirring the pudding for half an hour or so, which uncle George good-humouredly does, to the vociferous delight of the children and servants. The evening concludes with a glorious game of blind-man's buff, in an early stage of which grandpapa takes great care to be caught, in order that he may have an opportunity of displaying his dexterity.

On the following morning, the old couple, with as many of the children as the pew will hold, go to church in great state: leaving aunt George at home dusting decanters and filling casters, and uncle George carrying bottles into the dining-parlour, and calling for corkscrews, and getting into everybody's way.

When the church-party return to lunch, grandpapa produces a small sprig of mistletoe from his pocket, and tempts the boys to kiss their little cousins under it – a proceeding which affords both the boys and the old gentleman unlimited satisfaction, but which rather outrages grandmamma's ideas of decorum, until grandpapa says, that when he was just thirteen years and three months old, HE kissed grandmamma under a mistletoe too, on which the children clap their hands, and laugh very heartily, as do aunt George and uncle George; and grandmamma looks pleased, and says, with a benevolent smile, that grandpapa was an impudent young dog, on which the children laugh very heartily again, and grandpapa more heartily than any of them.

But all these diversions are nothing to the subsequent excitement when grandmamma in a high cap, and slate-coloured silk gown; and grandpapa with a beautifully plaited shirt-frill, and white neckerchief; seat themselves on one side of the drawing-room fire, with uncle George's children and little cousins innumerable, seated in the front, waiting the arrival of the expected visitors. Suddenly a hackney-coach is heard to stop, and uncle George, who has been looking out of the window, exclaims 'Here's Jane!' on which the children rush to the door, and helter-skelter down- stairs; and uncle Robert and aunt Jane, and the dear little baby, and the nurse, and the whole party, are ushered up-stairs amidst tumultuous shouts of 'Oh, my!' from the children, and frequently repeated warnings not to hurt baby from the nurse. And grandpapa takes the child, and grandmamma kisses her daughter, and the confusion of this first entry has scarcely subsided, when some other aunts and uncles with more cousins arrive, and the grown-up cousins flirt with each other, and so do the little cousins too, for that matter, and nothing is to be heard but a confused din of talking, laughing, and merriment.

A hesitating double knock at the street-door, heard during a momentary pause in the conversation, excites a general inquiry of 'Who's that?' and two or three children, who have been standing at the window, announce in a low voice, that it's 'poor aunt Margaret.' Upon which, aunt George leaves the room to welcome the new-comer; and grandmamma draws herself up, rather stiff and stately; for Margaret married a poor man without her consent, and poverty not being a sufficiently weighty punishment for her offence, has been discarded by her friends, and debarred the society of her dearest relatives. But Christmas has come round, and the unkind feelings that have struggled against better dispositions during the year, have melted away before its genial influence, like half-formed ice beneath the morning sun. It is not difficult in a moment of angry feeling for a parent to denounce a disobedient child; but, to banish her at a period of general good-will and hilarity, from the hearth, round which she has sat on so many anniversaries of the same day, expanding by slow degrees from infancy to girlhood, and then bursting, almost imperceptibly, into a woman, is widely different. The air of conscious rectitude, and cold forgiveness, which the old lady has assumed, sits ill upon her; and when the poor girl is led in by her sister, pale in looks and broken in hope – not from poverty, for that she could bear, but from the consciousness of undeserved neglect, and unmerited unkindness – it is easy to see how much of it is assumed. A momentary pause succeeds; the girl breaks suddenly from her sister and throws herself, sobbing, on her mother's neck. The father steps hastily forward, and takes her husband's hand. Friends crowd round to offer their hearty congratulations, and happiness and harmony again prevail.

As to the dinner, it's perfectly delightful – nothing goes wrong, and everybody is in the very best of spirits, and disposed to please and be pleased. Grandpapa relates a circumstantial account of the purchase of the turkey, with a slight digression relative to the purchase of previous turkeys, on former Christmas-days, which grandmamma corroborates in the minutest particular. Uncle George tells stories, and carves poultry, and takes wine, and jokes with the children at the side-table, and winks at the cousins that are making love, or being made love to, and exhilarates everybody with his good humour and hospitality; and when, at last, a stout servant staggers in with a gigantic pudding, with a sprig of holly in the top, there is such a laughing, and shouting, and clapping of little chubby hands, and kicking up of fat dumpy legs, as can only be equalled by the applause with which the astonishing feat of pouring lighted brandy into mince-pies, is received by the younger visitors. Then the dessert! – and the wine! – and the fun! Such beautiful speeches, and SUCH songs, from aunt Margaret's husband, who turns out to be such a nice man, and SO attentive to grandmamma! Even grandpapa not only sings his annual song with unprecedented vigour, but on being honoured with an unanimous ENCORE, according to annual custom, actually comes out with a new one which nobody but grandmamma ever heard before; and a young scapegrace of a cousin, who has been in some disgrace with the old people, for certain heinous sins of omission and commission – neglecting to call, and persisting in drinking Burton Ale – astonishes everybody into convulsions of

laughter by volunteering the most extraordinary comic songs that ever were heard. And thus the evening passes, in a strain of rational good-will and cheerfulness, doing more to awaken the sympathies of every member of the party in behalf of his neighbour, and to perpetuate their good feeling during the ensuing year, than half the homilies that have ever been written, by half the Divines that have ever lived.

Sketches by Boz, Charles Dickens, 1836

Chapter 1

Stir-up Sunday

Stir-up Sunday was the day that traditionally saw the cook – and indeed the whole Victorian family – in the kitchen making the pudding and cakes for Christmas. It was considered good luck for everyone to give the mixture and stir and make a wish of their own while doing so. So it would be logical to assume that is where the name 'stir-up Sunday' derives. In fact, it comes from the collect of the day that the Victorian family would have heard that morning in church: 'Stir up, we beseech thee, O Lord, the wills of thy faithful people, that they plenteously bringing forth the fruit of good works may of thee be plenteously rewarded.' This would sometimes

be parodied by the naughtier boy choristers to 'Stir up, we beseech thee, the pudding in the pot. And when we do get home tonight we'll eat it up hot.' The precise date of Stir-up Sunday changes year by year as it always falls on the last Sunday before Advent. Advent is based on Easter, which is the Church's principal movable feast, and an exact date is difficult for the layman to predict, but Stir-up Sunday has to fall some time during the second half of November. Christmas cakes and, especially Christmas or plum puddings, need at least six weeks to mature and yield their full flavour. And, in fact, many people would make two Christmas puddings at a time and leave one till the following year when it was thought to be much richer and more delicious.

Charms and trinkets-box

Making the Christmas pudding was not a purely culinary affair. It was hedged around with traditions and superstitions. The mixture would be stirred by everyone in the house, eyes closed while they made a wish. The stirring had to go in a clockwise direction or the wish would not be granted. During the stirring, the cook would add the charms that would be found in someone's piece of the pudding on Christmas Day. The usual trinkets included a ring, a coin (usually a silver farthing) and a thimble. When the diners ate their pudding, the one who found a ring could expect a wedding, the coin symbolised the gaining of wealth and the thimble meant – depending on the interpretation – either a life of blessedness or spinsterhood.

There is some debate over where the tradition of trinkets in the pudding began. The Victorians were certainly the first people to use them in the spherical Christmas pudding – as they invented it. However, the custom of hiding a charm in a cake is a pagan one and goes back to Twelfth Night Cake. The charm in Twelfth Night Cake was a bean and the lucky finder became the king of Twelfth Night – whereby hangs another tale to be told later in this book.

The Christmas Pudding

The Victorians invented, among so many other things, the muslin cloth. While this may seem small fry in comparison to the railways and the telephone, the muslin cloth nevertheless transformed nineteenth century cooking in the spherical shape of the pudding. While this could be sweet, in the modern sense of pudding, it could also be savoury – whatever the ingredients, the muslin cloth held the round pudding together while it steamed. But in both sweet and savoury puddings, suet was the vital ingredient and a particularly useful one for filling the hungry bellies of the poor.

In the less wealthy household, where meat was scarce, it was usual to have something filling before you reached the meat course. This was often a suet pudding or a Yorkshire pudding and it would take the edge off the appetite so that less meat would be needed. Mrs Gaskell's Mr Holbrook gave this view of domestic economy in her novel *Cranford*.

> When I was a young man, we used to keep strictly to my father's rule, 'No broth, no ball; no ball, no beef' and always began dinner with broth. Then we had suet puddings, boiled in the broth with the beef: and then we had the meat itself. If we did not sup our broth, we had no ball, which we liked a deal better; and the beef came last of all, and only those had it who had done justice to the broth and the ball.

By far the most long-lasting ball pudding of the Victorians was, though, the Christmas pudding which has retained its popularity to this day. They took older recipes – originally, it was a sloppy, porridgey dish – and made a solid pudding. They also took *out* one of the most important original ingredients – beef. Mincemeat and minced meat were in earlier times the same thing. Only during the nineteenth century did mincemeat come to refer to the dried fruit and spices that are the principal ingredient in mince pies. Early plum puddings used minced beef and mixed it with sugar, spices and dried fruit. The Victorians did, of course, keep the suet (as do most puddings today) as a binding ingredient. Suet is the raw animal fat that is usually found around the kidneys and so they did, in effect, keep some meat content in the recipe.

Or, rather, recipes. There are so many Victorian recipes for Christmas pudding from the great cookery writers of the day to every family's personal 'receipt'. Eliza Acton, possibly the greatest of the Victorian cookery writers, gave plenty of advice on 'boiled puddings'.

All the ingredients for puddings should be fresh and of good quality. It is a false economy to use for them such as have been too long stored, as the slightest degree of mustiness or taint in any one of the articles of which they are composed will spoil all that are combined with it. Eggs should always be broken separately into a cup before they are thrown together in the same basin, as a single very bad one will occasion the loss of many when this precaution is neglected. They should also be cleared from the specks with scrupulous attention, either with the point of a small three-pronged fork while they are in the cup, or by straining the whole through a fine hair-sieve after they are beaten. The perfect sweetness of suet and milk should be especially attended to before they are mixed into a pudding, as nothing can be more offensive than the first when it is over-kept, nor worse in its effect than the curdling of the milk, which is the certain result of its being ever so slightly soured.

Currants should be cleaned, and raisins stoned with exceeding care; almonds and spices very finely pounded, and the rinds of

oranges or lemons rasped or grated lightly off, that the bitter part of the skin may be avoided when they are used for this, or for any other class of dishes; if pared, they should be cut as thin as possible.

Plum-puddings, which it is customary to boil in moulds, are both lighter and less dry, when closely tied in stout cloths well buttered and floured, especially when they are made in part with bread; but when this is done, care should be taken not to allow them to burn to the bottom of the pan in which they are cooked; and it is a good plan to lay a plate or dish under them, by way of precaution against this mischance; it will not then so much matter whether they be kept floating or not. It is thought better to mix these entirely (except the liquid portion of them) the day before they are boiled, and it is perhaps an advantage when they are of large size to do so, but it is not really necessary for small or common ones.

A very little salt improves all sweet puddings, by taking off the insipidity, and bringing out the full flavour of the other ingredients, but its presence should not be in the slightest degree perceptible. When brandy, wine or lemon-juice is added to them it should be stirred in briskly, and by degrees, quite at last, as it would be likely otherwise to curdle the milk or eggs.

The author's (Eliza Acton's) Christmas pudding

To three ounces of flour, and the same weight of fine, lightly grated bread-crumbs, add six of beef kidney-suet, chopped small, six of raisins weighed after they are stoned, six of well-cleaned currants, four ounces of minced apples, five of sugar, two of candied orange-rind, half a teaspoonful of nutmeg mixed with pounded mace, a very little salt, a small glass of brandy, and three whole eggs. Mix and beat these ingredients well together, tie them tightly in a thickly-floured cloth, and boil them for three hours and a half. We can recommend this as a remarkably light small rich pudding.

From *Modern Cookery for Private Families* by Eliza Acton, 1845

A Real Christmas Pudding

I was lucky enough to discover the original handwritten 'receipt book' that belonged to my husband's great-great-grandmother. Being married to an Indian Army officer, she has a great number of recipes for dishes such as dhal, 'Indian cutlets' and, of course, curry. There are also many very British recipes, including at least four plum or Christmas puddings. This one, entitled 'A Real Xmas Pudding', appears opposite one for 'A Capital Cure for Boils'! Clearly a stout-hearted daughter of the empire had to battle on many fronts.

1 lb raisins, stoned and cut in half
1 lb currants picked, washed and dried
1 lb beef suet chopped fine
1 lb grated bread or 1/2 lb each grated bread and flour
8 eggs
1/4 lb sugar
1 salt spoon salt
1 tablespoon cinnamon and mace mixed
2 grated nutmegs
1 glass each of wine and brandy
another 1/4 lb sugar
1 pint milk

Prepare all the day before (except the eggs) that you may use them next morning. Beat the eggs lightly then put to them half the milk and beat together. Stir in the flour and bread then the sugar by degrees, then the suet and fruit (the fruit to be well floured to prevent its sticking). Stir hard. Now add the spice and liquor and the remainder of the milk. If it is not thick enough, add more bread or flour but if there is too much bread or flour the pudding will be heavy. Drop a cloth in boiling water, shake it out and sprinkle with flour. Lay it in a dish and pour in the pudding. Tie it tight, allowing for some swell. Boil for six hours. If you add grated lemon peel to the other ingredients it will much improve the pudding.

Christmas cake

While the Christmas pudding was based on a recipe that went back at least to medieval times, the Christmas cake was a Victorian invention in its entirety. Many of the ingredients are similar to those in plum pudding but without the alcohol – making it more suitable for a family tea – and solidified into cake form. Mrs Beeton has two Christmas cake recipes in her *Family Cookery* (a shorter version of the original *Household Management* of 1861). The first is the more familiar and not dissimilar to a modern-day recipe.

Christmas cake

1/2 a lb of butter, 1/2 a lb of castor sugar, 1/2 a lb of sultanas, 1/2 a lb of currants, 6 oz of mixed candied peel, 1 lb of flour, 1/4 oz baking-powder, 4 eggs, milk.

METHOD – Sieve the baking-powder 2 or 3 times with the flour on to a sheet of paper to mix well. Put the butter and the sugar into a clean pan and stand in front of the fire to soften. Weigh the fruit on to the flour, having carefully cleaned and picked them free from stalks and stones. Cut up the peel into thin shreds, and lay it with the fruit and flour. Break the eggs into a clean basin. Now proceed to beat up the butter and sugar into a cream with your hand, add the eggs one at a time, beating well after each addition of egg. When all are in, add the flour

and fruit, moisten to the usual cake batter consistency with milk, and bake in round or square well-papered and greased tins. This will make nearly 4 lb of cake, and can be baked in one or more cakes as desired.

TIME – From 3 to 4 hours to bake.

Mrs Beeton's second cake has some extra – and somewhat unexpected – ingredients, such as cream, treacle and vinegar. At first, the cake was simply decorated with holly but later it would be iced and decorated. Mrs Beeton offers various recipes, such as almond and sugar icing.

Sugar Icing for Cakes

INGREDIENTS – To every lb of loaf sugar allow the whites of 4 eggs and about 1 oz of fine starch.

METHOD – Beat the eggs to a stiff froth, and gradually sift in the sugar, which should be reduced to the finest possible powder, and gradually add the starch, also finely powdered. Beat the mixture well until the starch is smooth; then with a spoon or broad knife lay the icing equally over the cakes. These should then be placed in a very cool oven and the icing allowed to dry and harden, but not to colour. The icing may be coloured with strawberry or currant juice, or with prepared cochineal. If it be put on the cakes as soon as they are withdrawn from the oven the icing will become firm and hard by the time the cakes are cold. On very rich cakes, such as wedding, christening cakes, etc., a layer of almond icing is usually spread over the top, and over that the white icing as described. All iced cakes should be kept in a very dry place.

After that, more decorative icing could be added:

> Take an ordinary grocer's bag, place one of the piping funnels at
> the bottom, pour the prepared sugar into the bag and tear the
> paper off the point of it. Hold the bag in the right hand, and with
> the fingers of the left, squeeze the sugar through the funnel. The
> piping tubes have teeth, and patterns of piping vary according to
> the 'outlet'.

Generally, these cakes would be served simply from the cake stand with
perhaps a sprig of holly for decoration. After Mrs Beeton's death,
however, decoration became more commercialised. From the 1870s
onwards, specially made decorations, such as china Father Christmases,
would be placed on the cake.

Sweet poisons

We usually think of the Victorians as oblivious to the risk of rich foods – given the quantities they would regularly feast on. However, the Christmas cake, or plum cake, was banned from Eliza Acton's *Modern Cooking for Private Families* (1845). Her chapter on cakes begins:

> We have inserted here but a comparatively limited number of receipts for these 'sweet poisons' as they have been emphatically called, and we would willingly have diminished still further even the space which has been allotted to them, that we might have had room in their stead for others of a more really useful character; but we have felt reluctant to withdraw such a portion of any of the chapters as might materially alter the original character of the work, or cause dissatisfaction to any of our kind readers; we will therefore content ourselves with remarking that more illness is caused by habitual indulgence in the richer and heavier kinds of cakes that would easily be credited by persons who have given no attention to the subject.
>
> Amongst those which have the worst effects are almond, and plum pound cakes, as they are called; all varieties of the brioche and such others as contain a large quantity of butter and eggs.

Chapter 2

The Feast of St Nicholas

The 6 December is the Feast of St Nicholas, a saint whose real history – the little that is known of it – would seem to make him unlikely material for one of the best loved of all Christian saints. He was born in the city of Patara in Lycia in Asia Minor, a province of the Roman Empire in the Fourth Century. According to the inimitable Chambers' *Book of Days* (1869): 'So strong were his devotional tendencies, even from infancy, that we are gravely informed that he refused to suck on Wednesdays and Fridays, the fast-days

appointed by the church!' He became a monk, an abbot and eventually the archbishop of Myra and, though persecuted for his faith, was not actually martyred. He also became the patron saint of an extraordinarily diverse number of people including the Russian nation, virgins, children, Aberdeen, parish clerks, pawnbrokers, boatmen, fishermen, dockers, coopers, brewers, scholars, travellers, pilgrims, those who had unjustly lost lawsuits and even thieves.

His transformation into Father Christmas – aka Santa Claus – was a gradual one. Because of his own generosity (see St Nicholas – munificence and miracles), he was very much associated with the giving of presents. So on the eve of his feast day, children would put out hay and carrots for his horse and, in return, they would receive a present from him the next morning.

Present giving in the depths of winter was not just a Christian tradition. The Romans did the same thing during their Saturnalia festival and the Vikings' Woden would deliver presents in mid-winter, too. And, in Britain, there was the ancient character of Father Christmas, familiar from the mummers' plays. The Church pragmatically decided to continue the tradition but under the guardianship of a Christian saint. St Nicholas fitted the bill.

In fact, there was nothing very saintly about the earlier Father Christmas who was a drinker, fighter and lover! But the Victorians reinvented him, spliced him together with St Nicholas, changed his robe from pagan green to cheery red and brought in the reindeer and sleigh. The timing for the delivery of presents changed, too. Requests for presents by children were 'sent' by chimney post on 6 December to be delivered on the night of Christmas Eve.

St Nicholas – munificence and miracles

Two stories from his life explain how he became associated with both children and the giving of presents – which in turn were to make him the Christmas saint. Chambers again:

> A nobleman in the town of Patara had three daughters, but was sunk in such poverty, that he was not only unable to provide them with suitable marriage-portions, but was on the point of abandoning them to a sinful course of life from inability to preserve them otherwise from starvation. St Nicholas, who had inherited a large fortune, and employed it in innumerable acts of charity, no sooner heard of this unfortunate family, than he resolved to save it from the degradation with which it was threatened. As he proceeded secretly to the nobleman's house at night, debating with himself how he might best accomplish his object, the moon shone out from behind a cloud, and shewed him an open window into

which he threw a purse of gold. This fell at the feet of the father of the maidens, and enabled him to portion his eldest daughter. A second nocturnal visit was paid to the house by the saint, and a similar present bestowed, which procured a dowry for the second daughter of the nobleman. But the latter was now determined to discover his mysterious benefactor, and with that view set himself to watch. On St Nicholas approaching, and preparing to throw in a purse of money for the third daughter, the nobleman caught hold of the skirt of his robe, and threw himself at his feet, exclaiming: 'O Nicholas! Servant of God! Why seek to hide thyself?' But the saint made him promise that he would inform no one of this seasonable act of munificence.

From this incident in his life is derived apparently the practice formerly, if not still, customary in various parts of the continent, of the elder members and friends of a family placing, on the even of St Nicholas's Day, little presents, such as sweetmeats and similar gifts, in the shoes or hose of their younger relatives, who, on discovering them in the morning, are supposed to attribute them to the munificience of St Nicholas. In convents, the young lady-boarders

used, on the same occasion, to place silk-stockings at the door of
the apartment of the abbess, with a paper recommending themselves
to 'Great St Nicholas of her chamber.' The next morning they were
summoned together, to witness the results of the liberality of the
saint who had bountifully filled the stockings with sweetmeats...

The second legend ... A gentleman of Asia sent his two sons to
be educated at Athens, but desired them, in passing through the town
of Myra, to call on its archbishop, the holy Nicholas, and receive his
benediction. The young men, arriving at the town late in the evening,
resolved to defer their visit till the morning, and in the meantime took
up their abode at an inn. The landlord, in order to obtain possession
of their baggage, murdered the unfortunate youths in their sleep; and
after cutting their bodies to pieces, and salting them, placed the
mutilated remains in a pickling tub along with some pork, under the
guise of which he resolved to dispose of the contents of the vessel.
But the archbishop was warned by a vision of this horrid transaction,
and proceeded immediately to the inn, where he charged the
landlord with the crime.

The man, finding himself discovered, confessed his guilt, with great contrition to St Nicholas, who not only implored on his behalf the forgiveness of heaven, but also proceeded to the tub where the remains of the innocent youths lay in brine, and then made the sign of the cross and offered up a supplication for their restoration to life. Scarcely was the saint's prayer finished, when the detached and mangled limbs were miraculously reunited and, the two youths regaining animation, rose up alive in the tub, and threw themselves at the feet of their benefactor.

Christmas cards

A. HAPPY, NEW-YEAR

The Victorians invented the Christmas card. It all began with Henry Cole, the first director of the newly founded Victoria and Albert Museum. He commissioned the artist John Horsley who produced a triptych, the main picture of the archetypal Victorian family enjoying their Christmas together and on either side smaller panels featuring 'Clothing the Naked' and 'Feeding the Hungry' to remind the fortunate family of their Christian duties. Although Cole noted in his diary that he commissioned the design in 1843, it was not until 1846 that the card — 1,000 lithographed copies, all coloured by hand — was put on sale at Felix Summerly's Treasure House in London's

A MERRY Christmas.

wish you
a Merry
Christmas.

Bond Street, a shop in which Cole had an interest.

However, Cole has rivals for the crown of the inventor of the Christmas card. W. C. T. Dobson, a member of the Royal Academy, sent a Christmas sketch to a friend in 1844 and the following year lithographed it and sent it to all his friends. William Maw Egley produced a card in 1843 – or the unclear signature could have said 1848. And the Reverend Edward Bradley, a vicar from Newcastle, also made a card to send to his friends. None of these was for sale, however, so in terms of the first commercial Christmas card, that honour has to go to Henry Cole.

By the end of 1860s, cards had become immensely popular, especially
after the invention of the chromolithographic process meant that they
became much more affordable. Bells, cupids, Christmas puddings and lots
of snow were recurrent themes – and, of course, the robin with its bright
red breast became a particular symbol of Christmas, even though it was
resident all year round. Because of their red uniforms, Victorian postmen
were dubbed 'robin postmen'. They faced a mammoth task in the festive
season. The postmaster-general issued a special halfpenny
card stamp in 1870 but by 1880 was already begging the
public to 'post early for Christmas'.

Boy Bishops

The 6 December was also the date that
the Boy Bishop was elected and he
would hold his position from the Feast
of St Nicholas to the Feast of the
Holy Innocents, or Childermas Day,
on 28 December. In medieval times he
would be found in every cathedral and
many boys' schools. At Salisbury Cathedral,
the service of the Boy Bishop was printed and
set to music and, according to Chambers:

> It seems to have constituted literally a mimic transcript
> of the regular episcopal functions ... The actors in this solemn
> farce were composed of the choristers of the church, and must have
> been well drilled in the parts which they were to perform. The boy
> who filled the character of bishop, derived some substantial benefits
> from his tenure of office, and is said to have had the power of
> disposing of such prebends as fell vacant during the period of his
> episcopacy. If he died in the course of it, he received the funeral
> honours of a bishop, and had a monument erected to his memory, of
> which latter distinction an example may be seen on the north side
> of the nave of Salisbury Cathedral.

While the rise of Protestantism was to stamp out the practice in churches
and cathedrals, it survived into the Nineteenth Century in at least one

May the Christmas bells ring merrily to you.

WIRTHS BROTHERS
COPYRIGHT.

school, albeit somewhat changed in form. At Eton, the Eton Montem (literally translated from the Latin as 'to the mount') ceremony was celebrated in the early years of Victoria's reign. The scholars would dress in military rather than ecclesiastical uniforms, process to Salt Hill (the mount), dine and process back to Eton. During the procession boys in fancy dress would accost passers-by and demand tribute for their captain. They usually made a considerable sum, occasionally as much as £1,000 and the captain would have enough for his university career. The ceremony was finally abolished in 1847.

Salisbury Cathedral has recently revived the Boy Bishop and the head chorister ascends the Bishop's throne in a reconstruction of the medieval ceremony. According to the Cathedral it takes place: 'during the singing of the Magnificat with its revolutionary proclamation "God has put down the mighty from their throne and has exalted the humble and meek". The ceremony is a lesson in humility and recognition of the wisdom of youthful innocence.'

Chapter 3

Wassail, Wassail

As Christmas approached, so did the festive spirit. This took many forms – some of which had little to do with Christianity itself but rather harked back to earlier pagan practices.

St Thomas's Day

St Thomas's Day falls on 21 December, the shortest day of the year and the winter solstice. St Thomas himself – better known as doubting Thomas – was one of the apostles and his festival was instituted in the Twelfth Century. He is the patron saint of architects and builders and was asked to construct a palace finer than anyone had ever seen for the 'King of the Indies', Gondoforus. The king gave him an abundance of gold and silver and then travelled for two years while his palace was being built. Instead, St Thomas gave the king's wealth to the poor and sick and the king, on his return, sent him to prison while he decided on the most hideous form of death for disobeying his orders. He changed his mind when his brother who had recently died came back to life to tell the king that Thomas was a servant of God and should be spared. Thomas told him: 'Knowest thou not that they who would possess heavenly things have little care for the goods of this world! There are in heaven rich palaces without number, which were prepared from the beginning of the world for those who purchase the possession thereof through faith and charity.'

Because of the saint's charity to the poor, it became a custom that was still marked in Victorian times for the poor to 'go a-gooding' – that is to visit their richer neighbours on 21 December and beg money or provisions for Christmas. In different parts of the country, the practice was also known as 'mumping' or 'doleing'. In Staffordshire in 1857,

A MERRY CHRISTMAS IS THE LAY, THAT ROBINS CHIRP ON CHRISTMAS DAY

gooding was still going very strong. Old women and widows and representatives from every poor family would make their rounds, begging for alms. The clergyman was expected to give a shilling to everyone who came. Chambers notes that:

A liberal dole was distributed at the great house or the mansion of the principal proprietor in the parish; and at the kitchens of

all the squires and farmers' houses, tankards of spiced ale were
kept for the special refection of the red-cloaked old wives who
made in procession these foraging excursions on St Thomas's
Day. It is said that the hospitality shewn on such occasions
proved sometimes rather overpowering and the recipients of this
and other charitable benefactions found themselves occasionally
wholly unable to find their way back to their own habitations,
having been rendered, through the agency of John Barleycorn, as
helpless as the Wee bit Wilkie immortalised in Scottish song.

St Thomas grey, St Thomas grey
The longest night and the shortest day.

Wassail, wassail

Wassail was another pagan tradition that the Church took over. The word
comes from the Anglo Saxon 'wes hal' meaning literally 'be whole'. The
wassail itself was a bowl of steaming hot ale to which sugar, spices or the
soft pulp of roasted apples could be added. The bowl would be
processed around the parish – each house would be toasted and then
expected to replenish the stock of wassail. The Church glossed over
wassail's pagan origins, seeing it as a symbol of peace and goodwill

unto all men. The primmest of the
Victorians decided to change
its character still further and
call it the 'vessel cup' instead
of wassail cup thus giving it a
hint of the communion service.
However, it would still be taken
around from door to door,
accompanied by carol
singers and 'advent images'
– dolls representing the
Virgin Mary and Jesus – and
each household was
expected to make a
contribution to ensure their

good luck throughout the coming year.

The Victorians had a whole range of Christmas drinks, related to wassail, in that they were usually spicy, sweet and served hot. Wassail was based on ale but there was also mulled wine and punch that could combine wine with spirits. Eliza Acton in *Modern Cookery for Private Families* had several suggestions:

To mull wine

(An excellent French Receipt.)

Boil in a wineglassful and a half of water, a quarter of an ounce of spice (cinnamon, ginger slightly bruised, and cloves), with three ounces of fine sugar, until they form a thick syrup, which must not any account be allowed to burn. Pour in a pint of port wine, and stir it gently until it is on the point of boiling only: it should then be served immediately. The addition of a strip or two of orange-rind cut extremely thin, gives to this beverage the flavour of bishop. In France light claret takes the place of port wine in making it, and the better kinds of vin ordinaire are very palatable thus prepared.

Oxford Receipt for Bishop

Make several incisions in the rind of a lemon, stick cloves in these, and roast the lemon by a slow fire. Put small but equal quantities of cinnamon, cloves, mace and allspice, with a race of ginger, into a saucepan with half a pint of water: let it boil until it is reduced one-half. Boil one bottle of port wine, burn a portion of the spirit out of it by applying a lighted paper to the saucepan; put the roasted lemon and spice into the wine; stir it up well, and let it stand near the fire ten minutes. Rub a few knobs of sugar on the rind of a lemon, put the sugar into a bowl or jug, with the juice of half a lemon (not roasted), pour the wine into it, grate in some nutmeg, sweeten it to the taste, and serve it up with the lemon and spice floating in it.

Mrs Beeton offered another variation:

Punch, hot

¹/₂ a pint of brandy
¹/₂ a pint of rum
1 pint of boiling water
2 or 3 oz of loaf sugar
1 large lemon
a pinch of ground cinnamon
a pinch of grated nutmeg
a pinch of cloves

Remove the rind of the lemon by rubbing it with some of the sugar. Put the whole of the sugar, the cinnamon, nutmeg, cloves, brandy, rum and boiling water into a stewpan, heat gently by the side of the fire, but do not let it approach boiling point. Strain the lemon juice into a punch bowl, add the hot liquid and serve.

Christmas Carols and Waits

Although there are many Christmas carols that come from earlier or later periods, it was the Victorians who were to create — or recreate and embellish — most of those that remain favourites to this day.

A happy Christmas

Because the Victorians were great enthusiasts for parlour entertainment, carols such as 'Away in a Manger', 'God Rest Ye Merry Gentlemen', 'The First Noel', 'The Holly and the Ivy', 'It Came upon the Midnight Clear', 'Silent Night' and 'O Little Town of Bethlehem' would be sung by the entire family standing around the piano. Groups of singers would also sing in the streets or from house to house and this grew from a much older practice known as 'The Waits'.

The Waits originated in medieval times and there is some speculation as to their earliest beginnings. Were they a band of musical night watchmen? Did it refer to a group of woodwind instruments, precursors of the oboe? Were they a group of wandering Scottish minstrels? Whatever their origins, by Victorian times the Waits were groups of musicians who performed in the two to three weeks before Christmas, playing out of doors and usually going from house to house asking for donations. But they soon went from being the only authorised groups to one group of singers among many, much more ad hoc, bands of friends as Chambers points out:

> *Down to the year 1820, perhaps later, the waits had a certain degree of official recognition in the cities of London and Westminster. In London, the post was purchased; in Westminster,*

it was an appointment under the control of the High Constable
and the Court of Burgesses. A police inquiry about Christmas-
time, in that year, brought the matter in a singular way under
public notice. Mr Clay had been the official leader of the waits
for Westminster; and on his death, Mr Monro obtained the post.
Having employed a number of persons in different parts of the
city and liberties of Westminster to serenade the inhabitants,
trusting to their liberality at Christmas as a remuneration, he was
surprised to find that other persons were, unauthorised, assuming
the right of playing at night, and making applications to the
inhabitants for Christmas boxes. Sir R. Baker the police
magistrate, promised to aid Mr Monro in the assertion of his
claims; and the result, in several police cases, shewed that there

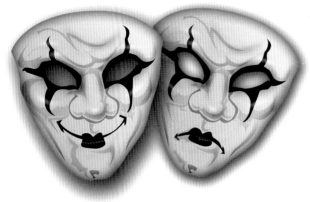

really was this vested right to charm the ears of the citizens of Westminster with nocturnal music. At present there is nothing to prevent any number of such itinerant minstrels from plying their midnight calling.

By the end of the Victorian era, more and more carollers appeared on the streets but, while their star rose, that of another even older tradition fell.

The Mummers

The last – and perhaps most interesting – of the groups of people who roamed the streets at Christmas, offering entertainment and asking for alms in return, were the mummers. As with the Waits, there is some confusion about their name. Theories include derivation from the Danish 'mumme' or the Dutch 'momme' meaning 'a mask' or simply from the mumbling sound of their speeches, coming as they did through the masks they wore.

The mummers were still thriving in early Victorian times but as the period went on the practice began to die out. They had something of the mystery play about them – but their origins were most certainly pagan rather than Christian. Chambers considers those origins to be the Roman Saturnalia, the midwinter festival that was to be replaced by Christmas, and celebrated by masquerading, dressing up and general merrymaking. There is more than a passing resemblance to the festivities of Mardi Gras before Lent and indeed, in medieval times, the mummers could perform from All Hallows Eve (31 October) all the way through to Easter. By the Nineteenth Century, however, they were very much a form of Christmas entertainment – though their performances were based on purely pagan themes.

In earlier times, there had been several popular legends and myths that were turned into mummers' plays but by the Victorian period there was mostly only one hero who took the lead: St George. He could also sometimes be called King George and would always have an evil foe – the

Turkish Knight or the Grand Turk (who had been particularly popular from the Crusades onwards). Other characters included quack doctors, lawyers, the parish beadle (a prototype policeman) and Father Christmas. There were many versions of the play in many dialects but the underlying story surely harked back to the ancient ceremonies of nature worship in which a

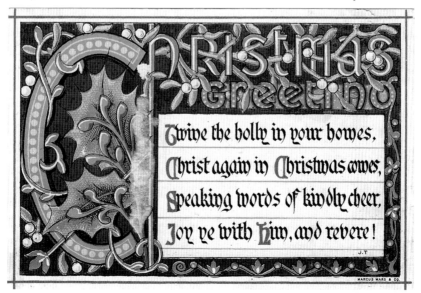

To Wish you a merry Christmas

victim (sometimes called the 'Year King') would be sacrificed to ensure the fertility of the crops in the coming year. His 'rebirth' would be represented by the choosing of a new 'Year King' the following spring. In the mummers' plays, this was transposed into a fight between St George and the Turkish Knight. St George would kill the knight but he would then be revived by the doctor – at which point all the mummers united in a request for alms.

A mummers' play

Chambers cites an entire mummers' play that was taking place in Tenby in south Wales in the 1860s. This play had three players, though there could be up to eight in other parts of the country. They all guarded their 'disguises' jealously. Mummers did not wear 'costumes' and the word 'disguise' was used meaningfully – it was bad luck to discover who was performing. Lines were kept equally secret. Nothing was written down but parts were handed on verbally often from father to son (there were no women in it either) and many local, topical references would sneak in, as would various corruptions of the original language.

Here are some of the highlights of the Tenby mummers' play.

FATHER CHRISTMAS enters carrying a holly bough

Here comes I, Old Father Christmas,
Christmas or not,
I hope Old Father Christmas
Will never be forgot.
A room – make room here, gallant boys,
And give us room to rhyme,
We're come to shew activity
Upon a Christmas time.
Acting youth or acting age,
The like was never acted on this stage;
If you don't believe what I now say,
Enter St George and clear the way.

SAINT GEORGE enters carrying a sword and spear

Here come I, St George, the valiant man,
With naked sword and spear in hand,
Who fought the dragon and brought him to
the slaughter,
And for this won the king of Egypt's
daughter.
What man or mortal will
dare to stand
Before me with my sword
in hand;
I'll slay him, and cur him as
small as flies,
And send him to Jamaica to
make mince-pies.

THE TURKISH KNIGHT enters carrying a sword

Here come I, a Turkish knight,
Draw out thy sword and fight.

They fight, the Turkish knight is slain and St George suffers remorse.

SAINT GEORGE

Ladies and gentlemen,
You've seen what I've done,
I've cut this Turk down
Like the evening sun;
Is there any doctor that can be found,
To cure this knight of his deadly wound?

DOCTOR enters

Here come I, a doctor,
A ten pound doctor;
I've a little bottle in my pocket,
Called hokum, shokum, alicampane;
I'll touch his eyes, nose, mouth and chin,
And say: "Rise, dead man" and he'll fight again.

SAINT GEORGE

Here am I, St George, with shining armour bright,
I am a famous champion, also a worthy knight,
Seven long years in a close cave was kept,
And out of that into a prison leaped,
From out of that into a rock of stones,
There I laid down my grievous bones
Many a giant did I subdue,
And ran a fiery dragon through.
I fought the man of Tillotree,
And still will gain the victory.
First, then, I fought in France,

> *Second, I fought in Spain,*
> *Thirdly, I came to Tenby,*
> *To fight the Turk again.*

They fight again with the same result. The Turkish knight is again revived
by the doctor who then assumes a new character.

OLIVER CROMWELL

> *Here come I, Oliver Cromwell,*
> *As you may suppose,*
> *Many nations have I conquered,*
> *With my copper nose.*
> *I made the French to tremble,*
> *And the Spanish for to quake,*
> *I fought the jolly Dutchmen,*
> *And made their hearts to ache.*

BEELZEBUB enters

> *Here come I, Beelzebub,*
> *Under my arm I carry a club,*
> *Under my chin I carry a pan,*
> *Don't I look a nice young man?*

Then one of the players brings the proceedings to the point of the play.

> *Ladies and gentlemen,*
> *Our story is ended,*
> *Our money box is recommended;*
> *Five or six shillings will not do us harm,*
> *Silver, or copper, or gold if you can.*

Parlour entertainment

Of course, fashions changed considerably during the Victorian period and much of this earlier, perhaps rather religiously dubious, entertainment fell from favour. Chambers explains it thus:

> *The rude and irreverent mysteries and miracle plays which delighted our ancestors, have been succeeded in the gradual course of improvement by the elaborate stage mechanism and display of our own times; and the coarse drolleries which characterized the old Christmas festivities, have made way for the games and charades, and other refined amusements of modern drawing-rooms.*

So, while so many entertainments – Waits, wassailers, carollers, mummers – would often still come to the Victorian family's door, the family itself was more than able to provide plenty of its own amusement. Almost every family had a piano and several members able to play it. Other popular instruments included violins, flutes and harps – so musical evenings, often with singing and dancing, were commonplace. And, while this kind of parlour entertainment would have been popular all of the year, at Christmas it had a particular importance. As with so many Victorian 'traditions', Charles Dickens played a large part in establishing it.

Christmas was certainly a time that Victorian families would gather together – as we do today. And Dickens celebrated this image repeatedly in his Christmas stories, particularly *Household Words* and *All the Year Round*. In these stories, families and friends would

congregate around a roaring fire – perhaps not surprisingly in those cold and draughty Nineteenth Century houses. The company would sing, perform music and plays, mime (charades were popular), read poetry and tell stories. Sometimes, the stories would have a religious theme but the Victorians simply adored anything with fairies or goblins, ghosts and mysteries. The first English translation of *Grimms' Fairy Tales* appeared in 1823 and Charles Kingsley, Christina Rossetti and Lewis Carroll were all popular. The most famous Victorian ghost story of them all, though was, of course, Dickens' own much-loved morality tale.

A Christmas Carol

A Christmas Carol is so well known it hardly needs to be re-told. Suffice it to say that, during the course of his conversion from lonely, cold-hearted miser to generous family man, Scrooge meets the Ghost of Christmas Present, (the second spirit to visit him on Christmas Eve) who more closely resembles Father Christmas's earlier rather disreputable pagan image than the more respectable red-clad figure of the end of the Victorian era.

It was his own room. There was no doubt about that. But it had undergone a surprising transformation. The walls and ceiling were so hung with living green, that it looked a perfect grove; from every part of which bright gleaming berries glistened. The crisp leaves of holly, mistletoe, and ivy reflected back the light as if so many little mirrors had been scattered there; and such a mighty blaze went roaring up the chimney as that dull petrification of a hearth had never known in Scrooge's time, or Marley's, or for many and many a winter season gone. Heaped up on the floor, to form a kind of throne, were turkeys, geese, game, poultry, brawn, great joints of meat, sucking-pigs, long wreaths of sausages, mince-pies, plum-puddings, barrels of oysters, red-hot chestnuts, cherry-cheeked apples, juicy oranges, luscious pears, immense twelfth-cakes, and seething bowls of punch, that made the chamber dim with their delicious steam. In easy state upon this couch there sat a jolly Giant, glorious to see; who bore a glowing torch, in shape not unlike Plenty's horn, and held it up, high up, to shed its light on Scrooge as he came peeping round the door.

'Come in!' exclaimed the Ghost. 'Come in! and know me better, man!'

Scrooge entered timidly, and hung his head before this Spirit. He was not the dogged Scrooge he had been; and though the Spirit's eyes were clear and kind, he did not like to meet them.

'I am the Ghost of Christmas Present,' said the Spirit. 'Look upon me!'

Scrooge reverently did so. It was clothed in one simple deep green robe, or mantle, bordered with white fur. This garment hung so loosely on the figure, that its capacious breast was bare, as if disdaining to be warded or concealed by any artifice. Its feet, observable beneath the ample folds of the garment, were also bare; and on its head it wore no other covering than a holly wreath, set here and there with shining icicles. Its dark-brown curls were long and free; free as its genial face, its sparkling eye, its open hand, its cheery voice, its unconstrained demeanour, and its joyful air. Girded round its middle was an antique scabbard; but no sword was in it and the ancient sheath was eaten up with rust.

Chapter 4

Deck the Halls

It is widely accepted that when Prince Albert married Victoria he brought with him numerous German Christmas traditions including, most famously, the decorated Christmas tree. It is perhaps less well known that it was the English cleric St Boniface who, in the Eighth Century, had introduced the idea of the Christmas tree to the Germans when he went there to preach the gospel. Of course, long before Prince Albert, English homes had been decorated for the festive season. The main decorations were woodland greenery – holly, ivy, mistletoe – all of them belonging to much earlier pre-Christian traditions and all of which were still widely used in Victoria's reign.

Mistletoe was, of course, the plant most revered by the Druids and it played a major part in their winter solstice celebrations. The chief druid would cut the mistletoe with a golden knife, caught in a white cloth by other druids or, according to some traditions, by virgins in white vestments, after which a pair of white bulls would be sacrificed. The plant was then divided up among the people who hung it above their doors. Kissing under the mistletoe is a solely British custom but the kisses were limited. Each time a kiss was taken, a berry was plucked from the mistletoe. When there were no more berries, there was no more kissing.

May joy and peace with you abide This coming happy Christmas-tide.

Mistletoe was always regarded as a pagan plant by the Church and so it was never used in decorating churches at Christmas, though it was always a popular plant in the home. Holly and ivy were equally pagan. The Roman Saturnalia – the midwinter festival – used them as decoration for the house or as gifts or good luck charms to friends and neighbours. Holly was also believed to be a protection against witchcraft, while ivy was a symbol of immortality. The Christian Church nevertheless absorbed them both into their own traditions even associating holly with Christ's crown of thorns. Christmas decorations were not put up until Christmas Eve, as it was considered bad luck to do it any earlier. Great quantities of holly, ivy and mistletoe were cut down and dispatched to London and other cities.

A Merry Christmas to You.

The Yule Log

Before Queen Victoria and Prince Albert popularised the Christmas tree,
there was the ancient custom of the Yule Log. It had both Scandinavian
and Celtic origins. At the feast of Juul at the winter solstice, the
Scandinavians would burn a great log in honour of the god Thor; the Celts
held perpetual fire to be sacred and it was imperative that the log was
kept burning, preferably at least until Twelfth Night when Christmas
officially ended. The Church took the Yule Log under its aegis, too,
declaring it should be made of ash wood as it was a fire of ash made by
the shepherds beside which the infant Jesus was first washed and
dressed. The shepherds had had to use ash, it was explained, as it is the
only wood that will burn well while it is still green and it did, in fact,
become the traditional wood for the Yule Log in England, though in
Scotland it was usually birch.

The most important factor in the Yule Log was its size. As it had to burn
for many days, it was basically as big as your fireplace could take.
According to Chambers:

> The bringing in and placing of the ponderous block on the hearth of
> the wide chimney in the baronial hall was the most joyous of the
> ceremonies observed on Christmas Eve in feudal times. The
> venerable log, destined to crackle a welcome to all-comers was

drawn in triumph from its resting-place at the feet of its living brethren of the woods. Each wayfarer raised his hat as it passed, for he well knew that it was full of good promises and that its flame would burn out old wrongs and heart churnings, and cause the liquor to bubble in the wassail bowl, that was quaffed to the drowning of ancient feuds and animosities.

Even the ashes left after the fire had finally burned out had their uses, including a cure for toothache, added fertility for the crops and as a general protection or good luck charm for the home. It was thought best, though, to have some of the original log remaining so that it could be stored for the following Christmas when it would be used to help light the new Yule Log. This would ensure that the house would not burn down during the intervening period. There was, however, also the possibility of bad luck related to the Yule Log, if a squinting or bare-footed person or a flat-footed woman entered when the log was burning.

O Christmas Tree!

The decorated Christmas tree was a long-standing German tradition when Prince Albert brought it to England in 1841. Queen Victoria wrote of its effect on her family:

Today I have two children of my own to give presents to, who, they know not why, are full of happy wonder at the German Christmas tree and its radiant candles... [The Christmas tree] quite affected dear Albert who turned pale, and had tears in his eyes, and pressed my hand very warmly.

The idea spread rapidly from Windsor Castle to the rest of the country and within a matter of a decade, the Christmas tree had become a British tradition, too. Presents and edible treats were hung on the boughs and candles made everything glitter. The decorations were, in fact, elaborate and many were home made. Tin soldiers, whistles and little trinkets would be hidden among the branches and catch the flickering candlelight. Useful, home-made gifts, such as mittens for children would be hung up. A Christmas doll, angel or star adorned the top of the tree.

Much of the decoration was home made, often by children. Garlands were popular and could be wound round and round the tree. You could string anything Christmassy on them – nuts, dried fruit, pine cones, pieces of holly or ivy, berries of all kinds. Ribbons, painted paper flowers and gilded pine cones all added colour. Strong Christmassy scents contributed greatly to the atmosphere, such as sticks of cinnamon or oranges stuck with cloves. But, above all, there was the seasonal smell of gingerbread, sweets and lots of other edible treats that were made in the family kitchen and hung on the tree's boughs.

Charles Dickens's Christmas Tree

I have been looking on, this evening, at a merry company of children assembled round that pretty German toy, a Christmas tree. The tree was planted in the middle of a great round table, and towered high above their heads. It was brilliantly lighted by a multitude of little tapers; and everywhere sparkled and glittered with bright objects. There were rosy-cheeked dolls, hiding behind the green leaves; and there were real watches (with movable hands, at least, and an endless capacity of being wound up) dangling from innumerable twigs; there were French-polished tables, chairs, bedsteads, wardrobes, eight-day clocks, and various other articles of domestic furniture (wonderfully made, in tin, at Wolverhampton), perched among the boughs, as if in preparation for some fairy housekeeping; there were jolly, broad-faced men, much more agreeable in appearance than many real men – and no wonder, for their heads took off, and showed them to be full of sugar-plums; there were fiddles and drums; there were tambourines, books, word-boxes, paint-boxes, sweetmeat boxes, peep-show boxes, and all kinds of boxes; there were trinkets for the elder girls, far brighter than any grown-up gold and jewels; there were baskets and pin-cushions in all devices; there were guns, swords and banners; there were witches standing in enchanted rings of pasteboard, to tell fortunes; there were tetotums, humming-tops, needle-cases, pen-wipers, smelling-bottles, conversation-cards, bouquet-holders; real fruit, made artificially dazzling with gold leaf; imitation apples, pears, and walnuts, crammed with surprises; in short, as a pretty child, before me delightfully whispered to another pretty child, her bosom friend, 'There was everything, and more.'

Charles Dickens *A Christmas Tree* in *Household Words*, 1850

Gingerbread and other sweet treats

Gingerbread and biscuits cut into such shapes as hearts, stars and trees – and, of course, gingerbread men – all to be used as decorations for the Christmas tree, as well as for tea-time treats, were another German tradition that arrived in England with Prince Albert, and in America with the German immigrants at around the same time. Gingerbread was already well established by the time Eliza Acton was cooking and writing and she had several recipes for gingerbread.

Thick, light gingerbread

Crumble down very small, eight ounces of butter into a couple of pounds of flour, then add to, and mix thoroughly with them, half a pound of good brown sugar, two ounces of powdered ginger, and half an ounce of ground caraway-seeds; beat gradually to these, first two pounds of treacle, next three well-whisked eggs and last of all half an ounce of carbonate of soda dissolved in a very small cupful of warm water; stir the whole briskly together, pour the mixture into very shallow tins, put it immediately into a moderate oven, and bake it for an hour and a half. The gingerbread thus made will be remarkably light and good. For children part of the spice and butter may be omitted.

Other of Miss Acton's gingerbread recipes added grated lemon rind or coconut. Mrs Beeton, on the other hand, preferred golden syrup.

Gingerbread honeycomb

¹/₂ a lb of flour
¹/₄ of a lb of the coarsest brown sugar
¹/₂ a lb of golden syrup
¹/₄ of a lb of butter
1 dessertspoonful of allspice
2 tablespoonfuls of ground ginger
the peel of ¹/₂ a lemon grated
   and the whole of the juice

Mix all these ingredients together, forming a paste sufficiently thin to spread upon baking sheets. Beat it well, grease the tins and spread the paste very thinly over them; bake it in a rather slow oven, and watch it until it is done; withdraw the tins, cut the gingerbread into pieces about 4 inches square with a knife, and roll each piece round the fingers as it is raised from the tin. About ¹/₂ an hour, sufficient for 4 dozen squares.

My husband's great-great-great-grandmother had her own sub-continental version of gingerbread that contains a measurement – a chuttock – I have never found the meaning of but must be some kind of scoop, perhaps an Indian one.

Gingerbread receipt

8 chuttocks of flour
8 chuttocks of sugar
6 chuttocks of butter
2 chuttocks of pounded ginger
4 chuttocks of sucka (treacle)
4 chuttocks of orange marmalade
1 nutmeg

1 tablespoonful of allspice and one of cloves

There were other recipes for biscuits (or cookies) with different flavours that could be hung on the tree. Spices such as cinnamon, caraway and yet more ginger were popular, as were additional ingredients, especially nuts and dried fruits. Mrs Beeton suggests coconut, lemon and almond in the shape of macaroons.

Coconut biscuits

10 oz of castor sugar
2 whites of eggs
6 oz of desiccated coco-nut

Beat the whites of eggs to a stiff froth, add the other ingredients and form into pyramids; place the pyramids on paper, put the paper on tins and bake the biscuits in rather a cool oven until they are just coloured a light brown.

Lemon biscuits

$^3/_4$ of a lb of flour
6 oz of castor sugar
3 oz of fresh butter
2 eggs
the grated rind of a lemon
1 dessertspoonful of lemon juice

Rub the butter into the flour, stir in the castor sugar and very finely minced lemon peel, and when these ingredients are thoroughly mixed, add the eggs, which should be previously well whisked and the lemon juice. Beat the mixture well for a few minutes, then drop it from a spoon on to a greased tin, about 2 inches apart, as the biscuits will spread when they get warm; place the tin in the oven, and bake the biscuits to a pale brown from 15 to 20 minutes.

Macaroons

6 oz of ground sweet almonds
8 oz of castor sugar
the whites of 2 eggs
wafer-paper

Mix the sugar and ground almonds well together on the board, then put them into a mortar, add the whites of eggs and proceed to rub the mixture well into a smooth paste. When it begins to get stiff and stands up well it is ready, or if uncertain whether the paste has been pounded enough, try one in the oven, and if all right, lay sheets of wafer-paper over clean baking sheets and lay out the biscuits upon it with a spoon, or savoy bag, place a few split almonds on the top of each, then bake in a cool oven.

Candy

The Victorian kitchen would have been busy in the weeks before Christmas making all kinds of candies and sweets that would hang on the tree as well as being little gifts. Turning sugar into candy was, however, quite a complicated process. Eliza Acton tried to clarify it thus:

> The technicalities by which confectioners distinguish the different degrees of sugar-boiling, seem to us calculated rather to puzzle than to assist the reader, and we shall, therefore, confine ourselves to such plain English terms as may suffice, we hope, to explain them. After having boiled a certain

time, the length of which will in a measure depend upon the quality of the sugar as well as on the quantity of water added, it becomes a thin syrup, and will scarcely form a short thread if a drop be pressed between the thumb and finger and they are then drawn apart; from five to ten minutes more of rapid boiling will bring it to a thick syrup, and when this degree is reached the thread may be drawn from one hand to the other at some length without breaking; but its appearance in dropping from the skimmer will perhaps best denote its being at this point, as it hangs in a sort of string as it falls. After this the sugar will soon begin to whiten, and to form large bubbles in the pan, when, if it be intended for barley-sugar, or caramel, some lemon juice or other acid must be added to it, to prevent its graining or becoming sugar again; but if wanted to candy, it must be stirred without ceasing until it rises almost to the top of the pan, in one large white mass, when it must be used immediately or laded out into paper cases or on to dishes, with the utmost expedition, as it passes in an instant almost, from this state to one in which it forms a sort of powder, which will render it necessary to add water, to stir it until dissolved, and to reboil it to the proper point. For barley sugar likewise it must be constantly stirred, and carefully watched after the lemon juice is added. A small quantity should be dropped from time to time into a large basin of cold water by those who are inexperienced in the process; when in falling into this it makes a bubbling noise, and if taken out immediately after, it snaps clean between the teeth without sticking to them it must be poured out instantly: if wanted for sugar-spinning, the pan must be plunged as quickly as possible into a vessel of cold water.

After this the sugar was used to make sweets of all kinds. It could be chopped into bite-sized pieces or twisted into shapes, the most popular of which was perhaps the cane – did it represent a shepherd's crook or the letter 'J' for Jesus? No one can be sure. Comfits were a favourite sweet, often with a seed, especially caraway seed, coated in hard sugar. They were known for sweetening the breath and so were sometimes called 'kissing comfits'. Sugar plums (one of the Victorian candies we all know the name of because of Tchaikovsky's Sugar Plum Fairy) were not plums at all but comfits made of boiled sugar with an aniseed or caraway seed at the centre and made in an assortment of colours and flavours in the shape of a plum with a little wire 'stalk' at the top – making them very convenient for hanging on the tree.

Eliza Acton in *Modern Cookery for Private Families* has a whole chapter on confectionary:

Barley-sugar

Add to three pounds of highly refined sugar one pint and a quarter of spring water, with sufficient white of egg to clarify it … pour to it, when it begins to whiten, and to be very thick, a dessertspoonful of the strained juice of a fresh lemon; and boil it very quickly … A few drops of essence of lemon may be added to it, just as it is taken from the fire. Pour it on to a marble slab, or on to a shallow dish which has been slightly oiled, or rubbed with a particle of fresh butter; and when it begins to harden at the edges form it into sticks, lozenges, balls, or any other shapes at pleasure. While it is still liquid it may be used for various purposes, such as Chantilly baskets, palace bonbons, *croquantes* (these are formed of small cakes, roasted chestnuts, and various other things, just dipped singly into the barley-sugar and then arranged in good form and joined in a mould), *cerises* [cherries] *au caramel* etc.

Best sugar, 3lbs; water, 1^{1}/4 pint; white of egg, ^{1}/4 of 1; lemon-juice, 1 dessertspoonful.

Orange-flower candy

Beat in three-quarters of a pint, or rather more, of water, above the fourth part of the white of an egg, and pour it on two pounds of the best sugar broken into lumps. When it has stood a little time, place it over a very clear fire, and let it boil for a few minutes, then set it on one side, until the scum has subsided; clear it off, and boil the sugar until it is very thick, then strew in by degrees three ounces of the *petals* of the orange-blossom, weighed after they are picked from their stems. Continue to stir the candy until it rises in the white mass in the pan then lay it, as quickly as it can be done in cakes with a large spoon, upon thick and very dry sheets of writing paper placed quite flat upon the backs of dishes or upon trays. Take it off when it is entirely cold, and lay the candy reversed upon dishes, or place the cakes on their edges round the rim of one until they are perfectly cold; then secure them from the air without delay in close shutting tin boxes or canisters. They will remain excellent for more than a year.

Sugar, 2lbs; water, $^3/_4$ pint; $^1/_4$ white of egg; orange blossom, 3oz.

Palace Bonbons

Take some fine fresh candied orange-rind, or citron, clear off the sugar which adhere to it, cut it into inch-squares, stick these singly on the prong of a silver fork or on osier-twigs, dip them into liquid barley-sugar, and place them on a dish rubbed with the smallest possible quantity of very pure salad oil. When cold, put them into tin boxes or canisters well dried, with paper, which should also be very dry, between each layer.

A magazine of the time suggested: 'A dainty conceit is to line a number of

small sweet-grass baskets with pretty lace doilies, fill with choice bonbons and ornament neatly with scarlet satin ribbon tied in a large, graceful bow; place a sprig of bright holly in some of these bows and mistletoe in others.'

Mince pies

Without doubt, however, the Christmas sweetmeat *par excellence* was the mince pie. Custom had it that if you ate one mince pie on each of the twelve days of Christmas, preferably each one made by a different person, you would have good luck for the next twelve months. Mince pies were made from mincemeat which originally was minced meat, just as it was similarly used for Christmas pudding. By Victorian times, certainly late Victorian times, though, the meat content was represented usually by suet alone mixed with fruits, nuts, sugar and spices. Eliza Acton has one traditional recipe for mincemeat that includes ox tongue or sirloin and another more modern one, that has suet alone. Mrs Beeton has a variety of mincemeat recipes, all of them omitting meat except for suet.

Mincemeat

1 lb of finely chopped suet
1 lb of currants washed and picked
1 lb of raisins stoned and quartered
1 lb of chopped apples
1 lb of castor sugar
$^1/_2$ a lb of sultanas
$^1/_4$ of a lb of shredded, mixed candied peel
2 lemons
$^1/_2$ a gill of brandy
$^1/_2$ a saltspoonful each of nutmeg, mace and cinnamon

Pare the lemons thinly, simmer the rinds in a little water until perfectly tender, then pound them or rub them through a fine sieve. Mix all the ingredients well together, press into a jar, cover closely and keep in a cool, dry place for at least a month before using.

Mrs Beeton, *Family Cookery*

Mince pies royal

Add to half a pound of good mincemeat an ounce and a half of pounded sugar, the grated rind and the strained juice of a large lemon, one ounce of clarified butter, and the yolks of four eggs; beat these well together, and half fill, or rather more, with the mixture, some pattypans lined with fine paste [pastry]; put them into a moderate oven, and when the insides are just set, ice them quickly with the whites of the eggs beaten to snow, and mixed quickly at the moment with four heaped tablespoonsful of pounded sugar; set them immediately into the oven again, and bake them slowly of a fine light brown.

Mincemeat, $^1/_2$ lb; sugar $1^1/_2$ oz; rind and juice, 1 large lemon; butter, 1 oz; yolks, 4 eggs. Icing: whites, 4 eggs; sugar, 4 tablespoonsful.

Eliza Acton, *Modern Cookery for Private Families*

Christmas games

Away from the frost, the fog and the often bitter cold of December nights, all of the family gathered at home for Christmas around that blazing Victorian hearth. Once there, they would sing carols, read stories or – one of the favourite pastimes on the night before Christmas – they would play games. The Victorians loved parlour games, though Chambers points out that in this they were not dissimilar to their forebears.

He quotes an earlier writer on the subject of Christmas entertainments:

> *Dancing is one of the chief exercises or else there is a match at Blindman's Buff or Puss in the Corner. The next game is Questions and Commands, when the commander may oblige his subjects to answer any lawful question, and make the same obey him instantly, under the penalty of being smutted [having the face blackened], or paying such forfeit as may be laid on the aggressor. Most of the other diversions are cards and dice.*

From the above, we gather that the sports on Christmas evenings, a hundred and fifty years ago, were not greatly dissimilar to those in vogue at the present day. The names of almost all the pastimes then mentioned must be familiar to every reader, who has probably also participated in them himself at some period of his life. Let us only add charades, that favourite amusement of modern drawing-rooms (and of these only the name, not the sport itself, was unknown to our ancestors), together with a higher spirit of refinement and delicacy, and we shall discover little difference between the juvenile pastimes of a Christmas party in the reign of Queen Victoria, and a similar assemblage in the reign of Queen Anne or the first Georges. One favourite Christmas sport, very generally played on Christmas Eve, has been handed down to us from time immemorial under the name of 'Snapdragon'. To our English readers this amusement is perfectly familiar, but it is almost unknown in Scotland, and it seems therefore desirable here to give a description of the pastime.

A quantity of raisins are deposited in a large dish or bowl (the broader and shallower this is, the better), and brandy or some other spirit is poured over the fruit and ignited. The bystanders now endeavour, by turns, to grasp a raisin, by plunging their hands through the flames; and as this is somewhat of an arduous feat, requiring both courage and rapidity of action, a considerable amount of laughter and merriment is evoked at the expense of the unsuccessful competitors. While the sport of Snapdragon is going on, it is usual to extinguish all the lights in the room, so that the lurid glare from the flaming spirits may exercise to the full its weird-like effect. There seems little doubt that in this amusement we retain a trace of the fiery ordeal of the middle ages and also of the Druidical fire-worship of a still remoter epoch.

Christmas Eve supper

Though a feast was to come the next day, the Victorians enjoyed a substantial meal, too, on Christmas Eve. Once the family had arrived, it was unlikely they would venture out on to the freezing streets again that night – midnight mass was a service only held in Catholic churches in the Nineteenth Century. So, after the games had been played and the carols sung, a late supper would be laid out for the adults. *The Delineator* magazine suggested the following as ideal for the occasion:

> *For this festive occasion have a chafing dish arranged ready for use, a cut-glass punch bowl and ladle, a Santa Claus in a sleigh drawn by reindeer. Asparagus, maiden hair or other ferns, to represent a forest, will supply further decoration. An ideal Christmas Eve supper may comprise caviar sandwiches, devilled oysters, creamed sweetbreads, cold boned turkey, lettuce salad, cheese and coffee. A claret punch made of claret, sherry, dices of cucumber, mint, lemon, orange and other fruits may be served in the glass punch bowl.*

The Night Before Christmas

'Twas the night before Christmas, when all through the house
Not a creature was stirring, not even a mouse;
The stockings were hung by the chimney with care,
In hopes that St Nicholas soon would be there;
The children were nestled all snug in their beds,
While visions of sugar-plums danced in their heads;
And mamma in her 'kerchief, and I in my camp,
Had just settled our brains for a long winter's nap,
When out on the lawn there arose such a clatter,
I sprang from the bed to see what was the matter.
Away to the window I flew like a flash,
Tore open the shutters and threw up the sash.
The moon on the breast of the new-fallen snow,
Gave the lustre of mid-day to objects below,
When, what to my wondering eyes should appear,
But a miniature sleigh, and eight tiny reindeer,
With a little old driver, so lively and quick,
I knew in a moment it must be St Nick.
More rapid than eagles his coursers they came,
And he whistled, and shouted, and called them by name;
'Now Dasher! Now, Dancer! Now Prancer and Vixen!
On, Comet! on Cupid! On Donner and Blitzen!
To the top of the porch! To the top of the wall!
Now dash away! Dash away! Dash away all!'
As dry leaves that before the wild hurricane fly,
When they meet with an obstacle, mount to the sky;
So up to the house-top the coursers they flew,

A Christmas
fraught
with Joys divine dear friend
be thine.

With the sleigh full of toys, and St Nicholas too.
And then, in a twinkling, I heard on the roof,
The prancing and pawing of each little hoof.
As I drew in my head and was turning around,
Down the chimney St Nicholas came with a bound.
He was dressed all in fur, from his head to his foot,
And his clothes were all tarnished with ashes and soot.
A bundle of toys he had flung on his back,
And he looked like a pedlar, just opening his pack.
His eyes – how they twinkled! His dimples how merry!
His cheeks were like roses, his nose like a cherry!
His droll little mouth was drawn up like a bow,
And the beard of his chin was as white as the snow;
The stump of a pipe he held tight in his teeth,
And the smoke it encircled his head like a wreath;

He had a broad face and a little round belly,
That shook when he laughed, like a bowlful of jelly.
He was chubby and plump, a right jolly old elf,
And I laughed when I saw him, in spite of myself;
A wink of his eye and a twist of his head,
Soon gave me to know I had nothing to dread.
He spoke not a word, but went straight to his work,
And filled all the stockings; then turned with a jerk,
And laying his finger aside of his nose,
And giving a nod, up the chimney he rose;
He sprang to his sleigh, to his team gave a whistle,
And away they all flew like the down of a thistle.
But I heard him exclaim, 'ere he drove out of sight,
'Happy Christmas to all, and to all a good-night.'
                    Clement Clark Moore (1779-1863) *The Night Before Christmas*

Chapter 5

𝕿𝖍𝖊 𝕭𝖔𝖆𝖗'𝖘 𝕳𝖊𝖆𝖉
𝖆𝖓𝖉 𝕺𝖙𝖍𝖊𝖗 𝕯𝖊𝖑𝖎𝖈𝖆𝖈𝖎𝖊𝖘

Christmas was the focal point of the entire year for most Victorians. Even that least sentimental of writers, Robert Chambers, softens his tone when writing of Christmas Day:

> At present, Christmas-day, if somewhat shorn of its ancient glories, and unmarked by that boisterous jollity and exuberance of animal spirits which distinguished it in the time of our ancestors, is,

The Birth of Christ   Die heilige Nacht

nevertheless, still the holiday in which of all others throughout the year, all classes of English society most generally participate. Partaking of a religious character, the forenoon of the day is usually passed in church, and in the evening the re-united members of the family assemble round the joyous Christmas-board. Separated as many of these are during the rest of the year, they all make an effort to meet together round the Christmas-hearth. The hallowed feelings of domestic love and attachment, the pleasing remembrance of the past, *and the joyous anticipation of the future, all cluster round these family-gatherings, and in the sacred associations with which they are intertwined, and the active deeds of kindness and benevolence which they tend to call forth, a realization may almost be found of the angelic message to the shepherds of Bethlehem – Glory to God in the highest, and on earth peace, good-will toward men.*

Nevertheless, he can't resist pointing out the festival's pagan origins:

Sir Isaac Newton, indeed, remarks in his Commentary on the Prophecies of Daniel, *that the feast of the Nativity, and most of the other ecclesiastical anniversaries, were originally fixed at cardinal points of the year, without any reference to the dates of the incidents which they commemorated, dates which, by the lapse of time, had become impossible to be ascertained. Thus the Annunciation of the Virgin Mary was placed on the 25th of March, or about the time of the vernal equinox; the feast of St. Michael on the 29th of September, or near the autumnal equinox; and the birth of Christ and other festivals at the time of the winter-solstice. Many of the apostles' days—such as St. Paul, St. Matthias, and others—were determined by the days when the sun entered the respective signs of the ecliptic, and the pagan festivals had also a considerable share in the adjustment of the Christian year.*

Christmas day in the morning

Breakfast, church and presents all featured in the Victorian Christmas Day morning and each family would have their own way of ordering them. Although there was a feast ahead, the Victorians did not stint on breakfast. The US *Delineator* magazine devised a 'Christmas breakfast for adults' – presumably, the children were too excited to eat:

> A basket in the shape of a horn of plenty may be used for a centrepiece, and it may be filled with fruits of the season. A circular lace cover, that reaches just to the edge of the table is employed. A good menu for a Christmas breakfast is baked apples with sweet cream, broiled smelts with sauce tartare, English mutton chops, creamed potatoes, ham omelette, Parker House rolls, buttered toast, griddle cakes with maple syrup, tea and coffee.

Victorian presents varied, of course, according to the wealth of the family but many of the gifts were made at home and had sentimental rather than monetary value. In poor households, a child's Christmas stocking – the idea became popular around 1870 – might contain some seasonal fruits

and some nuts. However, when the candles on the tree in one of the wealthier homes were lit, the children would rush in to discover what was waiting for them underneath it. In 1868, the American magazine, *Harper's Bazaar*, gave a lengthy list of gifts that might be suitable for every age group:

> For boys there are leaping-horses arranged on a platform in order not to injure the carpets; goats that bleat, and dogs that bark; menageries with all sorts of wild animals; fire-engines with hose that throw the water across a room; livery stables with vehicles, hostlers, and horses; grocery stores and restaurants; pack-mules with well-filled panniers, driven by Swiss muleteers; express-wagons heavily laden with boxes, barrels, and parcels; steamers, and craft of every nation; locomotive and train; canes, riding-whips etc – all exact imitations used by the grown folks every day before admiring boyish eyes.
>
> A very expensive present for a little girl is a miniature dinner-set of French china, ornamented with a painted wreath. In the same case with the china are cut-glass goblets, silver-ware, cutlery, bronze candelabras, and table linen – everything, indeed that the most fastidious little folks could desire for a bountifully spread table – all carefully packed away in an oaken chest. Another case contains a tiny and complete toilette set, brushes, combs, hand-glass, pomade-jar etc. Still another is a drawing-room with rosewood and brocatelle furniture; again there is a dining-room, a kitchen, an old-fashioned cupboard well supplied with crockery, and doll equipages of every kind, carriages, coupes, and sleighs. A useful present, called the Little Embroiderer, is a work-box furnished with worsteds, patterns, needles and simple directions for using them. A color-box is

supplied with paints, pallet and brushes. The Moss Rose Surprise-box is a bunch of roses and buds. As you stoop to smell the perfume a concealed spring opens the largest rose with a loud noise and a doll fairy flies at your face.

Other presents on offer that year included

'clowns performing most absurd antics, when turned by a crank; caricatures of Napoleon and Bismarck, apes black boots; Punch and Judy wrangling as usual; games of squails and parlor lotto; Chinese billiards and croquet for the floor and for the table; ruined castles and the Coliseum all to be rebuilt of blocks of wood; an improved kaleidoscope produces, as if by magic, the most beautiful pictures from common garden flowers. A handsome doll, possessed of a stately and dignified mien, dressed in the style of a French Marquise of the ancient regime; another is a younger lady with a pretty blonde face of wax, blue eyes of glass, yet not glassy, and golden curls of real hair, a dress of white poplin gored a la princesse, blue silk girdle, with reticule attached containing a tiny mouchoir and porte-monnaie; papal Zouaves, gay hussars, Swiss peasants and Russians clad in furs; angel dolls in cherub array; whole families of paper dolls, with mammas and daughters displaying the latest Paris fashions. The handsomest toy of the season, sold by-the-way at eighty-five dollars,

FATHER CHRISTMAS & HIS LITTLE FRIENDS. Nº 2   MARCUS WARD & CO

is in a rosewood box about two feet square. The front and top of glass disclose an amphitheatre filled with spectators and gayly dressed figures on the stage, above which is stretched a tight rope. On turning a crank at the side of the box music is heard – very sweet music, too, and played with good effect, for the figures on stage begin to dance in a frenzied manner, but in excellent time and a tiny Blondin appears on the tight-rope above, wheeling a barrow back and forth, amidst the fluttering of flags and tossing of caps in the audience. Hand-grenades that may be used in the parlor send out harmless missiles in every direction. Japanese lightning is an innocent kind of fireworks, the stick, held in the hand, sends out stars of fire through the room. Most curious of all is the Chinese wonder-paper for perfuming a room. Crimp a slip of the paper, set it on a table, and apply fire, instantly green grass an inch high springs up and a delicious odor is diffused through the apartment.

In 1873, the same magazine gave the following advice to wives contemplating buying Christmas presents for their husbands:

Gentlemen do not care for the pretty trifles and decorations that delight ladies; and as for real necessities, they are apt to go and buy anything that is a convenience just as soon as it is discovered. Knickknacks, articles of china, etc are generally useless to them. A Lady cannot give a Gentleman a gift of great value because he would certainly feel bound to return one still more valuable and thus her gift would lose all its grace and retain only a selfish commercial aspect.

What, then, shall she give? Here is the woman's advantage. She has her hands, while men must transact all their present giving in hard cash. She can hem fine handkerchiefs – and in order to give them intrinsic value, if their relationship warrants such a favor, she can embroider the name or monogram with her own hair. If the hair is dark it has a very pretty, graceful effect, and the design may be shaded by mingling the *different hair of the family. We knew a gentlemen who for years lost every handkerchief he took to the office; at length his wife marked them with her own hair, and he never lost another. Such gifts are made precious by love, time and talent.*

The bare fact of rarity can raise an object commercially valueless, to an aesthetic level. Souvenirs from famous places or of famous people, a bouquet of wild thyme from Mount Hymettus, an ancient Jewish shekel or Roman coin, etc. All such things are very suitable as presents to gentlemen and will be far more valued than pins, studs, etc which only represent a certain number of dollars and cents. Do not give a person who is socially your equal a richer present than he is able to give you. He will be more mortified than pleased. But between equals it is often an elegance to disregard cost and depend on rarity, because gold cannot always purchase it. Still between very rich people presents should also be very rich or else their riches are set above their friendship and generosity.

By 1896, however, *Harpers' Bazaar* gave a list of suitable presents for men that could be bought just one week before Christmas Day:

Everything for men this season in the way of gifts is leather but instead of the accompanying prunella, silver takes its place. The English goods are very attractive, and the leading American manufacturers have produced copies of these, and thus all the large shops are filled with many articles, any of which would delight the heart of a man. If one begins in silver, it is necessary to note that repousse work has gone out of fashion as far as presents for the sterner sex are concerned, and everything must be solid, simple and handsome. In inkstands there are many elaborate affairs in crystal and cut glass with silver stoppers, plain and highly polished and silver trays to be placed underneath

them. Silver seals, silver mucilage-pots, silver pen-racks, silver pen-holders, silver pen-tweezers, small silver stamp-boxes for the waistcoat pocket. Paperweights assume the guise of animals, and those in bronze are actual works of art. For the table – and a bachelor would appreciate this, especially if he is keeping bachelor's hall – there are heavy crystal decanters of the Queen Anne pattern. Silver coasters for decanters are also acceptable presents but one gift always appreciated is a silver cigarette or cigar lamp. Waistcoat-pocket editions of everything are in vogue and the most fashionable leathers are taken from the monkey, the elephant, the snake, and the pig. There still remain many other pretty presents, any of which is appropriate for a man, without resorting to the work-basket or the embroidery-frame.

Dickens' presents

Charles Dickens wrote of the moment of present giving:

But now a knocking at the door was heard, and such a rush immediately ensued that she with laughing face and plundered dress was borne towards it the centre of a flushed and boisterous group, just in time to greet the father, who came home attended by a man laden with Christmas toys and presents. Then the shouting and the struggling, and the onslaught that was made on the defenceless porter! The scaling him with chairs for ladders to dive into his pockets, despoil him of brown-paper parcels, hold on tight by his cravat, hug him round his neck, pommel his back, and kick his legs in irrepressible affection! The shouts of wonder and delight with which the development of every package was received! The terrible announcement that the baby had been taken in the act of putting a doll's frying-pan into his mouth, and was more than suspected having swallowed a fictitious turkey, glued on a wooden platter! The immense relief of finding this a false alarm! The joy, and gratitude, and ecstasy! They are all indescribable alike. It is enough that by degrees the children and their emotions got out of the parlour, and by one stair at a time, up to the top of the house; where they went to bed, and so subsided.

Church and charity

It wasn't, though, just to each other that the Victorian family gave presents. They knew it was also their Christian duty to give to the poor and Christmas was a time when charity was a priority. The middle classes were advised to do their duty – all year round, but at Christmas more so than ever – by everyone from the Church to Mrs Beeton. She instructed:

A Happy Christmas

Charity and Benevolence are duties which a mistress owes to herself as well as to her fellow creatures; and there is scarcely any income so small but something may be spared from it, even if it be but 'the widow's mite'. It is always to be remembered, however, that it is the spirit of charity which imparts to the gift a value beyond its actual amount, and is by far its better part ... Visiting the houses of the poor is the only practical way really to understand the actual state of each family. Great advantages may result from visits paid to the poor; for there being, unfortunately, much ignorance, generally amongst them with respect to all household knowledge, there will be opportunity for advising and instructing them, in a pleasant and unobtrusive manner, in cleanliness, industry, cookery and good management.

Chambers, too, comments on charity at Christmas:

From the Queen downwards, all classes of society contribute their mites to relieve the necessities and increase the comforts of the poor, both as regards food and raiment. Even in the work-houses –

those abodes of short-commons and little ease – the authorities, for once in the year, become liberal in their housekeeping, and treat the inmates on Christmas-day to a substantial dinner of roast-beef and plum-pudding...Beggars, too, have a claim on our charity at this season...They may at least have their dole of bread and meat; and to whatever bad uses they may possibly turn our bounty, it is not probable that the deed will ever be entered to our discredit in the books of the Recording Angel.

At church – and many Victorian middle class families would wait until after the service to exchange presents – the service was dominated by carols and the Victorians loved them. According to Chambers:

Christmas ✠ Greeting ✠✠

Amid so many popular customs at Christmas, full of so much sweet and simple poetry, there is perhaps none more charming than that of the Christmas carols, which celebrate in joyous and yet devout strains the Nativity of the Saviour. The term is believed to be derived from the Latin cantare (to sing), and rola! an interjection expressive of joy. The practice appears to be as ancient as the celebration of Christmas itself, and we are informed that in the early ages of the church, the bishops were accustomed to sing carols on

Christmas-day among their clergy.

Christmas carols are sung on Christmas Eve as well as on the morning of Christmas-day, and indeed the former is regarded by many as the more appropriate occasion. Then the choristers, attached to the village-church, make their rounds to the principal houses throughout the parish, and sing some of those simple and touching hymns. The airs to which they are sung are frequently no less plaintive and melodious than the words, and, are often accompanied by instruments. The writer retains a vivid recollection of a carol which he heard sung, some years ago, on Christmas Eve by a detachment of the village choir, in front of a country-house in Devonshire, where he was at the time a visitor. The sweet and pathetic melody, which was both remarkably well sung and played, the picturesqueness of the group of singers, whose persons were only rendered visible, in the darkness of the night, by the light of one or two lanterns which they carried, and the novelty and general interest of the scene, all produced an impression which was never to be forgotten. These Christmas-eve carols are very general in Devonshire, and the usual custom for the singers is to club the money; which they receive on such occasions, and expend it in a social merry-making on Twelfth Day, a fortnight afterwards.

The Victorian Christmas Cookbook

But, of course, the whole day was moving Church and carols, charity and presents, towards its centrepiece – Christmas dinner. The feast itself would focus on a bird – usually a goose – though towards the end of Victoria's reign, the turkey became popular and a common sight before the holiday was a parade of turkeys wearing leather bootees that had walked the 80 miles from Norfolk to London. It was also quite common at the beginning of the period, and especially in the north of the country, that roast beef would be eaten instead. But whatever the main meat or fowl, this choice was only the beginning. There were also game pies, tongue, fish, pork, hams, beef and, for royal tables only, roasted swan. (Wild swans are all the property of The Crown and cannot be caught without permission for use in recipes.) There were strange composite dishes with one fowl stuffed inside another and huge game pies that included several types of bird with venison and hare. Even the poor would feast either on a bird or rabbit, usually cooked in the local baker's oven and carried home hot through the streets.

At refined tables, the meal might begin, though, with a clear soup, such as a consommé, served with oyster rolls. One of the most popular Nineteenth Century soups was turtle. Turtles were transported in fresh water tanks, alive, from the West Indies and weighed in at 60 to 100 pounds. The soup itself was made from the head and lights, while the belly, boiled, and the back, roasted, were served separately. Even the fins made a separate little dish, served in a rich sauce.

As turtles are now an endangered species, this recipe is included for historical interest only.

Turtle soup

$^1/_4$ lb of the best sun-dried turtle
$^1/_2$ a small tin of turtle fat (this may be omitted)
$^1/_4$ lb of lean neck of beef
$^1/_4$ lb of lean veal
the white and shell of 1 egg
3 quarts of good stock

1 onion
1 carrot
$^1/_2$ a turnip
a small strip of celery
a bouquet-garni (parsley, thyme, bay-leaf, basil, marjoram)
6 peppercorns
1 clove
a small blade of mace (tied in muslin)
1 glass of sherry (optional)
1 dessertspoonful of lemon juice
salt

Soak the turtle for 3 days, changing the water frequently. Put the stock, turtle, and a teaspoonful of salt into a stewpan and bring to the boil, then add the prepared vegetables, herbs, bag of peppercorns etc. and when the stock boils remove the scum as it rises. Put on the cover and cook gently for about 8 or 9 hours, adding more stock if that in the pan reduces very much. Strain, put the pieces of turtle aside and remove the fat from the soup when cold. Pass the beef and veal 2 or 3 times through the mincing machine, and add them together with the shell and stiffly whisked white of the egg to the soup, and whisk until it boils. Simmer gently for about $^1/_2$ an hour, then strain and return to the stewpan with the turtle and turtle fat cut into small squares, adding sherry, if used, lemon juice, and the necessary seasoning, and cook gently for a few minutes. Lemons cut in quarters are sometimes handed separately with this soup for those who prefer a strong flavour of lemon.

Mrs Beeton *Family Cookery*

Mock turtle soup

While turtle soup proper was popular in the early years of Victoria's reign, it was mock turtle soup that became the most popular soup of the day as the century went on. It was not for squeamish cooks as it involved working with various parts of a calf's head, amongst other time-consuming skills which a modern cook, even a highly accomplished one, would not normally be expected to do.

Oyster rolls

Oysters were extremely popular throughout the
Victorian period and were also quite
cheap – in *A Christmas Carol* Bob
Cratchit's goose is stuffed with
oysters. The following recipe is by
Mrs (Maria) Rundell, whose *A New
System of Domestic Cookery* first
appeared in 1805 but was to remain
in print until the 1880s; a best seller on
both sides of the Atlantic: 'Open them and save
the liquor; wash them in it, then strain it through a
sieve, and put a little of it into a tosser with a bit of butter and flour,
white pepper, a scrape of nutmeg, and a little cream. Stew them and cut
in dice; put them into rolls sold for the purpose.'

Consommé

The menu for Queen Victoria's Christmas dinner of 1899 can still be seen
in the Royal Collection. For her first course, she was served consommé.
Mrs Beeton has a recipe for 'Clear Soup' which is probably very similar.

3 pints of brown stock
$1/2$ lb of neck of beef (lean) finely chopped or passed two or three times
through the mincing machine
the whites and shells of 2 eggs
$1/2$ a carrot cut in two or three pieces
$1/2$ an onion
a small strip of celery
6 peppercorns
3 allspice
1 clove
salt

The stock should be cold and quite free from fat. Put it into a clean well-
tinned stewpan, add the vegetables, flavourings, seasonings, the shells of

MAY YOU ENJOY THE GENIAL
Xmas Feast.

the eggs crushed and the whites slightly whisked, and whisk all together over a gentle fire until just on boiling point, then let it simmer about $1/2$ an hour. Strain through a clean, dry cloth, re-heat and season to taste before serving. Half a glass of sherry, a teaspoonful of French vinegar or lemon juice and a small pinch of castor sugar, are frequently added when re-heating.

After the soup, a light fish course would follow, possibly with two dishes so that diners could choose a little of each.

Soles stewed in cream

Prepare some very fresh middling sized soles with exceeding nicety, put them into boiling water slightly salted, and simmer them for two minutes only. Lift them out, and let them drain. Lay them into a wide stewpan with as much sweet rich cream as will nearly cover them. Add a good seasoning of pounded mace, cayenne pepper and salt. Stew the fish softly from six to ten minutes or until the flesh parts readily from the bones. Dish them, stir the juice of half a lemon to the sauce, pour it over the soles, and send them immediately to table.

Eliza Acton *Modern Cookery for Private Families*

Lobster salad

1 hen lobster
lettuces, endive, small salad (whatever is in season)

a little chopped beetroot
2 hard-boiled eggs
a few slices of cucumber
For dressing:
4 tablespoonfuls of oil
2 tablespoonfuls of vinegar
1 teaspoonful of made mustard
the yolks of 2 eggs
cayenne and salt to taste
1/4 of a teaspoonful of anchovy
sauce

The ingredients for the dressing
should be mixed perfectly
smooth, and form a creamy
sauce.
Wash the salad, and thoroughly
dry it by shaking it in a cloth. Cut up the lettuces and endive, pour the
dressing on them, and lightly mix it in the small salad. Blend all well
together with the meat of the lobster. Pick the meat from the claws, cut
it up into nice square pieces, put half in the salad, and reserve the other
half for garnishing. Separate the yolks from the whites of 2 hard-boiled
eggs, chop the whites finely, and rub the yolks through a sieve. Arrange
the salad lightly on a glass dish, and garnish, first with a row of sliced
cucumber, then with the pieces of lobster, the yolks and whites of the
eggs, coral and beetroot placed alternately, and arrange in small separate
groups, so that the colours contrast nicely.

Mrs Beeton *Family Cookery*

After this, in the finest households, there might be yet another course
before the main one arrived. In Queen Victoria's 1899 Christmas menu it
was a light chicken dish, described as the 'entrée'.
Eliza Acton similarly describes the following dish as an 'entrée'.

Scallops of fowl au bechamel

Raise the flesh from a couple of fowls … and take it as entire as possible from either side of the breast; strip off the skin, lay the fillets flat, and slice them into small thin scallops; dip them one by one into clarified butter, and arrange them evenly in a delicately clean and not large frying pan; sprinkle a seasoning of fine salt over, and just before the dish is wanted for table, fry them quickly without allowing them to brown; drain them well from the butter, pile them in the centre of a hot dish, and sauce them with some boiling béchamel. This dish may be quickly prepared by taking a ready-dressed fowl from the spit or stewpan and by raising the fillets, and slicing the scallops into the boiling sauce before they have had time to cool.

Roast goose

The goose was certainly the most favoured fowl for the season at the beginning of Victoria's reign. This is Eliza Acton's recipe.

After it has been plucked and singed with care, put into the body of the goose two parboiled onions of moderate size finely chopped, and mixed with half an ounce of minced sage leaves, saltspoonful of salt, and half as much black pepper, or a proportionate quantity of cayenne; to these add a small slice of fresh butter. Truss the goose, and after it is on the spit, tie it firmly at both ends that it may turn steadily, and that the seasoning may not escape; roast it at a brisk fire, and keep it constantly basted. Serve it with brown gravy, and apple or tomata [sic] sauce. When the taste is in favour of a stronger seasoning than the above, which occurs we apprehend but seldom, use raw onions for it and increase the quantity; but should one still milder be preferred, mix a handful of fine breadcrumbs with the other ingredients, or two or three minced apples. The body of a goose is sometimes filled entirely with mashed potatoes, which for this purpose ought to be boiled very dry, and well blended with two or three ounces of butter, or with some thick cream, some salt and white pepper or cayenne: to these minced sage and parboiled onions can also be added at pleasure. A teaspoonful of made mustard, half as much of salt, and small portion of cayenne, smoothly mixed with a glass of port wine, are sometimes poured into the goose just before it is served, through a cut made in the apron.

We extract, for the benefit of our readers, from a work in our possession, the following passage, of which we have had no opportunity of testing the correctness. 'Geese, with sage and onions, may be deprived of power to breathe forth any incense, thus: Pare from a lemon all the yellow rind, taking care not to bruise the fruit nor to cut it so deeply as to let out the juice. Place this lemon in the centre of the seasoning within the bird. When or before it is brought to the table, let the flap be gently opened, remove the lemon with a tablespoon; avoid breaking, and let it instantly be thrown away, as its white pithy skin will have absorbed all the gross particles which else would have escaped.

Mrs Beeton advises on the carving thus:

The breast of a goose is the part most esteemed, therefore when the bird is larger than is necessary to meet the requirements of one meal, it frequently happens that the carving is confined solely to the breast. The carver should, however, consult the tastes of those he is serving with reference to choice of parts, for the leg is sometimes preferred. A large number of slices may be cut off the breast, and as the wing is the part least esteemed, the flesh of the upper part of it may with advantage be included in the slices cut from the breast. When onion farce has been employed it is advisable to ascertain if it be agreeable to the taste of the person for whom the portion of goose is intended, for so many dislike the farce itself, although they may like the flavour imparted to the bird by its use. The directions given for carving a boiled fowl may be applied here, although greater force will most probably be required in detaching the various parts.

Roast turkey

As the Nineteenth Century progressed, the turkey became increasingly popular as the festive bird. Mrs Beeton's recipe is remarkably similar to one that would be used today.

1 turkey
1 to 2 lb of sausage meat
1 to $1^1/2$ lb of veal forcemeat
2 or 3 slices of bacon
1 pint of good gravy
bread sauce
fat for basting

Prepare and truss the turkey. Fill the crop with sausage meat, and put the veal forcemeat inside the body of the bird. Skewer the bacon over the breast, baste well with hot fat, and roast in a moderate oven from $1^1/2$ to $2^1/2$ hours, according to age and size of the bird. Baste frequently, and about 20 minutes before serving remove the bacon to allow the breast to brown. Remove the trussing strings, serve on a hot dish, and send the gravy and bread sauce to table in sauce boats.

Mrs Beeton's bread sauce and cranberry sauce are the accompaniments:

Bread sauce

$1/2$ a pint of milk
1 tablespoonful of cream
2 oz of freshly made breadcrumbs
$1/4$ of an oz of butter
1 very small peeled onion
1 clove
salt and pepper

Put the milk and onion, with the clove stuck in it, into a small saucepan and bring to the boil. Add the breadcrumbs, and simmer gently for about 20 minutes, then remove the onion, add salt and pepper to taste, stir in the butter and cream and serve.

Cranberry sauce

1 quart of cranberries
1 lb of sugar
1 pint of water

Pick the cranberries carefully, put them into a stewpan with the water, and cook slowly for about 1 hour or until reduced nearly to a pulp. Stir from time to time during the process, and when they are sufficiently cooked stir in the sugar and turn into a dish to cool.

Small boiled turkey

Alexis Soyer wrote for the less wealthy household in *A Shilling Cookery for the People*. This is his recipe for cooking the entire Christmas dinner around a boiled turkey:

> Put into the pot four quarts of water, three teaspoonfuls of salt, one of pepper, have the turkey ready stuffed; when the water boils put in the turkey and four pieces of salt pork or bacon, of about half a pound each or whole, if you prefer it; also add half a pound of onions, one of white celery, six peppercorns, a bunch of sweet herbs; boil slowly for one hour and a half, mix three ounces of flour with two ounces of butter; melt it in a small pan, add a pint of the liquor from the pot, and half a pint of milk, the onions and celery taken out of the pot, and cut up and added to it; boil for twenty minutes, until it is thickish; serve the turkey on a dish, the bacon separate, and pour the sauce over the bird. A turkey done in this way is delicious. With the liquor, in which you may add a little colouring, a vermicelli, rice, or clear vegetable soup can be made; skim off the fat and serve. The above with a plum pudding made the day before, and re-warmed in boiling water in the pot whilst eating the soup and turkey, and the addition of potatoes, baked in the

embers, under the grate, is a very excellent dinner, and can all be done with the black pot.

At the other end of the social spectrum, Queen Victoria's table not only had a choice of three main courses, including beef and pork, but also a buffet. This included a boar's head, game pie, woodcock pie, tongue, roast fowl, brawn and yet more beef. The queen's chef, Charles Elme Francatelli gave the following recipe for Christmas pie in his book *The Cook's Guide and Housekeeper and Butler's Assistant*:

Christmas pie

First, bone a fowl, a wild duck, a pheasant, and two woodcocks etc; and having spread them open on the table, season them with aromatic herbs, pepper and salt; garnish each with some forcemeat; sew them up with small twine, place them on a sautapan [sic] with a little clarified butter, and set them to bake in a moderate heat, until they are done through; when they must be withdrawn from the oven and put in the cool. Meanwhile, place the carcasses in a stewpan, with two calf's feet, carrot, celery, onion, a clove of garlic, two bay leaves, thyme, cloves, mace and a little salt; fill up with four quarts of water; boil, skim, and then set this by the side to continue gently boiling for three hours when it must be strained, freed from grease, and boiled down to a thin glaze, and kept in reserve. Make four pounds of hot-water paste and use this to line a raised pie mould; line the inside of the pie with some of the forcemeat; arrange the baked fowl, duck etc. in the centre, placing at the same time layers of forcemeat and seasoning, until the preparation is used up; put a cover of paste on the top; weld it all round; cut the edge even; pinch it with pastry-pincers; ornament the top with leaves of paste; egg it over, and bake the pie for about two hours and a half; and when it comes out of the oven pour in the game-glaze through a funnel; put it in the larder to get cold; and previously to sending it

to table, remove the lid, garnish the top with aspic jelly; place the
pie on a napkin, in its dish and ornament the base with a border of
fresh-picked parsley.

Note:- The addition of truffles would be an improvement.

Boar's head

The custom of serving up the ancient dish at Queen's College, Oxford, to a variation of the old carol, sprang, according to the university legend, from a valorous act on the part of a student of the college in question. While walking in Shotover forest, studying his Aristotle, he was suddenly made aware of the presence of a wild boar, by the animal rushing at him open-mouthed. With great presence of mind, and the exclamation, "Greacum est," [It's in Greek] the collegian thrust the philosopher's ethics down his assailant's throat, and having choked the savage with the sage, went on his way rejoicing. (Chambers)

The boar's head was a favourite centrepiece of the Victorian festive table. The head was pickled for a week after certain parts have been removed, such as the eyes and the brain. After pickling, the head was stuffed with a rich forcemeat containing the brains, herbs and other flavourings. It was then sewn up and boiled for around six hours, glazed and 'dressed' with prunes for the eyes, placed on a large dish, and given an Elizabethan ruff to complete the picture.

Tongue

For each very large tongue, mix with half a pound of salt two ounces of saltpetre and three quarters of a pound of the coarsest sugar; rub the tongues daily, and turn them in the pickle for five weeks, when they will be fit to be dressed or to be smoked.

When taken fresh from the pickle they require no smoking, unless they should have remained in it much beyond the usual time, or have been cured with a more than common proportion of salt; but when they have been smoked and highly dried, they should be laid for two or three hours into cold, and as much longer into tepid water, before they are dressed: if extremely dry, ten or twelve hours must be allowed to soften them, and they should always be brought very slowly to boil. Two or three carrots and a large bunch of savoury herbs, added after the scum is cleared off, will improve them. They should be simmered until they are extremely tender, when the skin will peel from them easily. A highly dried tongue of moderate size will usually require from three and a half to four hours' boiling: an unsmoked one about an hour less; and for one which has not been salted at all a shorter time will suffice.

Eliza Acton *Modern Cooking for Private Families*

Hunter's Beef

This is one of Mrs Beeton's recipes for a beef dish that is very much of the Victorian era.

For a round of beef weight about 24 lb allow
3 oz of saltpetre
3 oz of coarse sugar
1 oz of cloves
1 grated nutmeg
$^1/_2$ an ounce of allspice
1 lb of salt
$^1/_2$ a lb of bay-salt

Let the beef hang for 2 or 3 days and remove the bone. Pound the spices, salt etc. in the above proportions and let them be reduced to the finest powder. Put the beef into an earthenware pan, rub all the ingredients well into it, and turn and rub it every day for a little over a fortnight. When it has been sufficiently long in pickle, wash the meat, bind it up securely with string, and place it in a pan with $^1/_2$ a pint of water at the bottom. Mince some suet, cover the top of the meat with it, and over the pan put a common crust of flour and water; bake for about 6 hours and when cold, remove the paste. The gravy that flows from it should be saved, as it adds greatly to the flavour of hashes, stews, etc. The beef may be glazed and garnished with aspic jelly.

Pip's Christmas dinner

In Chapter Four of *Great Expectations*, Charles Dickens creates the most memorably awful Christmas dinner imaginable:

We were to have a superb dinner, consisting of a leg of pickled pork and greens, and a pair of roast stuffed fowls. A handsome mince-pie had been made yesterday morning (which accounted for the mincemeat not being missed), and the pudding was already on the boil. These extensive arrangements occasioned us to be cut off unceremoniously in respect of breakfast; 'for I ain't,' said Mrs Joe, 'I ain't a going to have no formal cramming and busting and washing up now, with what I've got before me, I promise you!'

So, we had our slices served out, as if we were two thousand troops on a forced march instead of a man and boy at home; and we took gulps of milk and water, with apologetic countenances, from a jug on the dresser. In the meantime, Mrs Joe put clean white curtains up, and tacked a new flowered-flounce across the wide chimney to replace the old one, and uncovered the little state parlour across the Passage, which was never uncovered at any other time, but passed the rest of the year in a cool haze of silver paper, which even extended to the four little white crockery poodles on the mantelshelf, each with a black nose and a basket of flowers in his mouth, and each the counterpart of the other. Mrs Joe was a very clean housekeeper, but had an exquisite art of making her cleanliness more uncomfortable and unacceptable than dirt itself. Cleanliness is next to Godliness, and some people do the same by their religion.

My sister having so much to do, was going to church vicariously; that is to say, Joe and I were going. In his working clothes, Joe was a well-knit characteristic-looking blacksmith; in his holiday clothes, he was more like a scarecrow in good circumstances, than anything else. Nothing that he wore then, fitted him or seemed to belong to him; and everything that he wore then, grazed him. On the present festive occasion he emerged from his room, when the blithe bells were going, the picture of misery, in a full suit of Sunday penitentials. As to me, I think my sister must have had some general idea that I was a young offender whom an Accoucheur Policeman had taken up (on my birthday) and delivered over to her, to be dealt with according to the outraged majesty of the law. I was always treated as if I had insisted on being born, in opposition to the dictates of reason, religion, and morality, and against the dissuading arguments of my best friends. Even

when I was taken to have a new suit of clothes, the tailor had orders to make them like a kind of Reformatory, and on no account to let me have the free use of my limbs.

Joe and I going to church, therefore, must have been a moving

spectacle for compassionate minds. Yet, what I suffered outside, was nothing to what I underwent within. The terrors that had assailed me whenever Mrs Joe had gone near the pantry, or out of the room, were only to be equalled by the remorse with which my mind dwelt on what my hands had done. Under the weight of my wicked secret, I pondered whether the Church would be powerful enough to shield me from the vengeance of the terrible young man, if I divulged to that establishment. I conceived the idea that the time when the banns were read and when the clergyman said, 'Ye are now to declare it!' would be the time for me to rise and propose a private conference in the vestry. I am far from being sure that I might not have astonished our small congregation by resorting to this extreme measure, but for its being Christmas Day and no Sunday.

Mr Wopsle, the clerk at church, was to dine with us; and Mr Hubble the wheelwright and Mrs Hubble; and Uncle Pumblechook (Joe's uncle, but Mrs Joe appropriated him), who was a well-to-do corn-chandler in the nearest town, and drove his own chaise-cart. The dinner hour was half-past one. When Joe and I got home, we found the table laid, and Mrs Joe dressed, and the dinner dressing, and the front door unlocked (it never was at any other time) for the company to enter by, and everything most splendid. And still, not a word of the robbery.

The time came, without bringing with it any relief to my feelings, and the company came. Mr Wopsle, united to a Roman nose and a large shining bald forehead, had a deep voice which he was uncommonly proud of; indeed it was understood among his acquaintance that if you could only give him his head, he would read the clergyman into fits; he himself confessed that if the Church was 'thrown open', meaning to competition, he would not despair of making his mark in it. The Church not being 'thrown open', he was, as I have said, our clerk. But he punished the Amens tremendously; and when he gave out the psalm — always giving the whole verse — he looked all round the congregation first, as much as to say, 'You have heard my friend overhead; oblige me with your opinion of this style!'

I opened the door to the company — making believe that it was a habit of ours to open that door — and I opened it first to Mr Wopsle, next to Mr and Mrs Hubble, and last of all to Uncle Pumblechook. N.B. I was not allowed to call him uncle, under the severest penalties.

'Mrs Joe,' said Uncle Pumblechook: a large hard-breathing middle-aged slow man, with a mouth like a fish, dull staring eyes, and sandy hair standing upright on his head, so that he looked as if he had just been all but choked, and had that moment come to; 'I have brought *you, as the compliments of the season — I have brought you, Mum, a bottle of sherry wine — and I have brought you, Mum, a bottle of port wine.'*

Every Christmas Day he presented himself, as a profound novelty, with exactly the same words, and carrying the two bottles like dumb-bells. Every Christmas Day, Mrs Joe replied, as she now replied, 'Oh, Un — cle Pum — ble — chook! This IS kind!' Every Christmas Day, he retorted, as he now retorted, 'It's no more than your merits. And now are you all bobbish, and how's Sixpennorth of halfpence?' meaning me.

We dined on these occasions in the kitchen, and adjourned, for the nuts and oranges and apples, to the parlour; which was a change very like Joe's change from his working clothes to his Sunday dress. My sister was uncommonly lively on the present occasion, and indeed was generally more gracious in the society of Mrs Hubble than in other company. I remember Mrs Hubble as a little curly sharp-edged person in sky-blue, who held a conventionally juvenile position, because she had married Mr Hubble — I don't know at what remote period — when she was much younger than he. I remember Mr Hubble as a tough high-shouldered stooping old man, of a sawdusty fragrance, with his legs extraordinarily wide apart: so that in my short days I always saw some miles of open country between them when I met him coming up the lane.

Among this good company I should have felt myself, even if I hadn't robbed the pantry, in a false position. Not because I was squeezed in at an acute angle of the table-cloth, with the table in my chest, and the Pumblechookian elbow in my eye, nor because I was not allowed to speak (I didn't want to speak), nor because I was regaled with the scaly tips of the drumsticks of the fowls, and with those obscure corners of pork of which the pig, when living, had had the least reason to be vain. No; I should not have minded that, if they would only have left me alone. But they wouldn't leave me alone. They seemed to think the opportunity lost, if they failed to point the conversation at me, every now and then, and stick the point into me. I might have been an unfortunate little bull in a Spanish arena, I got so smartingly touched up by these moral goads.

It began the moment we sat down to dinner. Mr Wopsle said grace

with theatrical declamation – as it now appears to me, something like a religious cross of the Ghost in Hamlet with Richard the Third – and ended with the very proper aspiration that we might be truly grateful. Upon which my sister fixed me with her eye, and said, in a low reproachful voice, 'Do you hear that? Be grateful.'

'Especially,' said Mr Pumblechook, 'be grateful, boy, to them which brought you up by hand.'

Chapter 6

Sweet Treats
and Small Bangs

Even after the vast quantities that could comprise the main part of the Christmas feast, there were still plenty of sweets and puddings to follow. These could follow on straightaway or there might be a much-needed pause for a little digestive time first. At this point there would be some time for more home made entertainment, such as carols or games. In grander houses, there might be fireworks and even if the average family could not quite afford those, the Victorians also invented that particularly festive, if short-lived, pleasure of the Christmas cracker.

The cracker was invented by a pastry cook called Thomas Smith. On holiday in Paris in 1840, he saw for the first time how the French wrapped up sweets in twists of coloured paper and decided to bring the idea to England. Over the next seven years, he added riddles and mottoes and, eventually, the bang by inserting the explosive strips of cardboard we know today. It was the crackle of a log as he threw it on to the fire that gave him the idea of the chemically impregnated strip that produced a minor explosion when pulled apart. It was the bang that formed the basis of his success and, once he had devised the idea, sales appropriately enough rocketed. He also put in such novelties as 'grotesque and artistic head dresses, masks, puzzles, games, conundrums, jewels, toys, bric-a-brac, fans, flowers, tiny treasures, Japanese curiosities, perfumery, scientific and musical toys and many other surprises.' An entire stocking full of presents, in fact.

Crackers and cosaques

Crackers were first known as 'cosaques' and Thomas Smith advertised them thus:

> Thomas Smith and Company have endeavoured by employing special artists to produce designs, the finest modern appliances to interpret their work, and combining Art with Amusement and Fun with refinement, to raise the degenerate cosaque from its low state of gaudiness and vulgarity to one of elegance and good taste. The Mottoes, instead of the usual doggerel, are graceful and epigrammatic, having been specially written for Tom Smith's Crackers by well known Authors, among whom may be mentioned the late Tom Hood Esq, Charles H. Ross Esq, Editor of 'Judy', Ernest Warren esq, Author of 'Four Flirts', 'Laughing Eyes' etc.'

London's freezing

It is not surprising that the Victorians were so adept at arranging indoor entertainment at Christmas and spending as much time as possible around a blazing fire. Temperatures were much lower than they are today and freezing fog, snow and ice awaited them outside. Chambers records in his 'Book of Days':

> The Christmas of 1860 is believed to have been the severest ever experienced in Britain. At nine o'clock in the morning of Christmas-day in that year, the thermometer, at the Royal Humane Society's Receiving House, in Hyde Park, London, marked 15° Fahrenheit, or 17° below the freezing-point, but this was a mild temperature compared with what was prevalent in many parts of the country during the preceding night. Mr. E. J. Lowe, a celebrated meteorologist, writing on 25th December to the Times, from his observatory at Beeston, near Nottingham, says: 'This morning the temperature at four feet above the ground was 8° below zero, and

on the grass 13.8° below zero, or 45.8° of frost. The maximum heat yesterday was only 2°, and from 7 P.M. till 11 A.M. the temperature never rose as high as zero of Fahrenheit's thermometer. At the present time (12.30 P.M.), the temperature is 7° above zero at four feet, and 2.5° above zero on the grass.'

Other observations recorded throughout England correspond with this account of the intensity of the cold, by which, at a nearly uniform rate, the three days from the 24th to the 26th December were characterized. The severity of that time must still be fresh in the memory of our readers. In the letter of Mr. Lowe, above quoted, he speaks of having: 'just seen a horse pass with icicles at his nose three inches in length, and as thick as three fingers.'

Those who then wore moustaches must remember how that appendage to the upper-lip became, through the congelation of the vapour of the breath, almost instantaneously stiff and matted together, as soon as the wearer put his head out of doors.

The Skating Clergyman

The Reverend Francis Kilvert kept a diary from 1870-79 in which he describes conditions in Wales exactly a decade after Chambers' 'severest' Christmas. It is a fascinating insight not just into the Victorian climate but to its social climate, too.

Sunday, Christmas Day

As I lay awake praying in the early morning I thought I heard a sound of distant bells. It was an intense frost. I sat down in my bath upon a sheet of thick ice which broke in the middle into large pieces whilst sharp points and jagged edges stuck all round the sides of the tub like chevaux de frise, not particularly comforting to the naked thighs and loins, for the keen ice cut like broken glass. The ice water stung and scorched like fire. I had to collect the floating

*pieces of ice and pile them on a chair before I could use the sponge
and then I had to thaw the sponge in my hands for it was a mass of
ice. The morning was most brilliant. Walked to the Sunday School with
Gibbins and the road sparkled with millions of rainbows, the seven
colours gleaming in every glittering point of hoar frost. The Church
was very cold in spite of two roaring stove fires. Mr V. preached and
went to Bettws.*

Monday, 26th December

*Much warmer and almost a thaw. Left Clyro at 11am. At Chippenham
my father and John were on the platform. After dinner we opened a
hamper of game sent by Venables, and found a pheasant, a hare, a
brace of rabbits, a brace of woodcocks and a turkey. Just like them,
and their constant kindness.*

Tuesday, 27th December

*After dinner drove into Chippenham with Perch and bought a pair
of skates at Benks for 17/6. Across the fields to the Draycot water
and the young Awdry ladies chaffed me about my new skates. I had
not been on skates since I was here last, five years ago, and was
very awkward for the first ten minutes, but the knack soon came
again. There was a distinguished company on the ice, Lady Dangan,*

Lord and Lady Royston and Lord George Paget all skating. Also Lord and Lady Sydney and a Mr Calcroft. I had the honour of being knocked down by Lord Royston, who was coming round suddenly on the outside edge. A large fire of logs burning within an enclosure of wattled hurdles. Harriet Awdry skated beautifully and jumped over a half sunken punt. Arthur Law skating jumped over a chair on its legs.

Wednesday, 28th December

An inch of snow fell last night and as we walked to Draycot to skate the snowstorm began again. As we passed Langley Burrell Church we heard the strains of the quadrille band on the ice at Draycot. The afternoon grew murky and when we began to skate the air was thick with falling snow. But it soon stopped and gangs of labourers were at work immediately sweeping away the new fallen snow and skate cuttings of ice. The Lancers was beautifully skated. When it grew dark the ice was lighted with Chinese lanterns and the intense glare of blue, green and crimson lights and magnesium riband made the whole place as light as day. Then people skated with torches.

Thursday, 29th December

Skating at Draycot again with Perch. Fewer people on the ice today. No quadrille band, torches or fireworks, but it was very pleasant, cosy and sociable. Yesterday when the Lancers was being skated Lord Royston was directing the figures. Harriet Awdry corrected him in one figure and he was quite wrong. But he immediately left the quadrille and sat down sulking on the bank, saying to one of his friends, 'Those abominable Miss Awdrys have contradicted me about the Lancers'. This was overheard and repeated to Harriet by a mutual friend and the next time she saw him she said meaningly, 'Lord Royston sometimes remarks are overheard and repeated', or something to that effect. However soon after he wanted to make it up and asked her to

skate up the ice hand in hand with him. 'Certainly not, Lord Royston,'
she said. Lady Royston skates very nicely and seems very nice. A
sledge chair was put on the ice and Lady Royston and Lady Dangan,
Margaret, Fanny, Maria and Harriet Awdry were drawn about in it by
turns, Charles Awdry pushing behind and Edmund and Arthur and
Walter pulling with ropes. It was a capital team and went at a
tremendous pace up and down the ice. A German ladies' maid from
Draycot House was skating and making ridiculous antics.

Table decoration

Tables were, of course, specially decorated for Christmas but the
Victorian table was as a matter of course heavily adorned all year round.
Mrs Beeton set the scene (and indeed the table) thus:

It should be borne in mind that table decorations are far more effective
if they are simple and not too varied. If the decorations are too heavy
the table soon assumes an overcrowded appearance, and the beauty
and effect of the scheme is at once lost. For a table laid for, say, six to
twelve guests, two to four flower vases or bowls, around which trails of
asparagus fern, smilax etc. are draped, four candlesticks and half a
dozen small silver dishes containing bon-bons, almonds and preserved
fruits will be found ample decoration. This is, of course, in addition to
the covers, cruets, napkins which will be laid in the ordinary way.

Flowers for decoration should be those which are not very
strongly scented. To some the perfume of such flowers as gardenias,

stephanotis, hyacinths and others is not offensive but to others the strong scent in a heated room, especially during dinner, is considered very unpleasant … It is a fashion to have a single colour for a dinner-table decoration, this being often chosen of the same tint as the hostess's dress…

Floating flower bowls are wide shallow bowls of crystal, coloured glass or pottery, black Wedgwood being very effective. Only a little water is placed in the bowls, and the flowers, having had their stalks cut off quite short, are floated on the water. A brightly coloured bird, dragonfly or butterfly may be fastened to the edge of the bowl, and will add greatly to the effect… Water-lilies, anemones, Christmas roses and such cup-shaped flowers are most suitable to this particular form of decoration. As table-cloths are not always in evidence on dinner tables, one of these floating flower bowls resting on a dainty lace mat on a beautifully polished table has a very pleasing effect.

A very effective table-centre is provided by an alabaster, crystal or coloured glass bowl or vase, in which an electric light bulb is placed. The soft hues that will radiate from the bowl render little need for any but very scanty additional decorations. Table-cloths may be 'electrified' so that electric candelabra, placed anywhere on the table may be illumined and many novel and ingenious effects may thus be obtained. Many hostesses, when giving a dinner-party, dispense with electric light or gas altogether and simply rely on the mellow and subdued light of candles. The effect is very pleasing but one word of warning – do not let the light be too dim, for very few people can enjoy a repast when they cannot see what they are eating! If the candle shades are made to harmonise with the other table decorations, the effect will be greatly enhanced.

Cape gooseberries, which provide such rich colour through the winter months, may be rendered yet more beautiful and lasting if dipped in a solution of gum-arabic and water, and then dried. No water should be placed in vases containing Cape gooseberries. At Christmas time no better decoration can be found than holly with plenty of red berries, ivy and mistletoe. Candlesticks with shades to match the holly berries are very effective, and a very pleasing and seasonable effect can be created by sprinkling some of the twigs and foliage with artificial frost, which is easily obtainable at any grocer's.

To ice evergreen

For decorating the dinner table, it was customary not simply to use all the festive greenery and berries but to 'ice' them so they looked as if they had been covered in frost.

Dissolve a pound of alum by boiling it in a gallon of water. Pour it into a deep vessel and as it cools the alum will be precipitated. Choose the lightest sprays, and hang them with the stems upwards in cords stretched across the top of the vessel so that they do not touch the bottom. They will attract the alum in the process of crystallization, like the threads in sugar candy. The warmer the solution they are put in the smaller will be the crystals attached to them, but care must be taken that it be not hot enough to destroy the leaves or fronds, and if there be any berries, like holly, it must be hardly lukewarm. The same solution warmed again will do two or three bouquets.

Mary Jewry *Warne's Model Cookery* 1869

The Final Course

The table could be laid afresh for the sweets and desserts course – because, even after all that feasting, the day's supply of food had not reached its conclusion. As well as the plum pudding, creams, jellies, sorbets and ices would make their way to the table, all decorated with ferns and greenery. Surprise nuts were a favourite – walnuts were split in half, the kernel removed and replaced with little gifts, then mixed with real walnuts in a bowl. Dishes of fruit, bonbons served in baskets with ivy twined around their handles, hot roasted chestnut served in folded napkins, little dishes of damson cheese and hot salted almonds, baskets of crystallised fruits would all appear and be arranged beautifully on a new damask table cloth. Finger glasses or bowls would be laid for each person and, according to Mrs Beeton, in winter they should have tepid water with a leaf of scented geranium or a small flower floating in them.

Orange isinglass jelly

To render this perfectly transparent the juice of the fruit must be filtered, and the isinglass clarified; but it is not usual to take so much trouble for it. Strain as clear as possible, first through a sieve or muslin, then through a thick cloth or jelly bag, one quart of China orange-juice, mixed with as much lemon-juice as will give it an agreeable degree of acidity, or with a small proportion of Seville orange-juice. Dissolve two ounces and a half of isinglass in a pint of water, skim it well, throw in half a pound of sugar, and a few strips of the orange-rind, pour in the orange-juice, stir the

whole well together, skim it clean without allowing it to boil, strain it through a cloth or through a muslin many times folded, and when nearly cold put it into the moulds. This jelly is sometimes made without any water, by dissolving the isinglass and sugar in the juice of the fruit.

Eliza Acton *Modern Cookery for Private Families*

(Isinglass is a form of gelatine, made from fish gut. All gelatines are derived from animals. Calves' feet were the most popular providers of the necessary jelly to make the dessert set [as they still often do today]. Jellies could also be made from ground horn from deer.)

Fancy jellies

Transparent jelly is shown to much advantage, and is particularly brilliant in appearance, when moulded in shapes, which are now very commonly used for the purpose. The centre spaces can be filled, after the jelly is dished, with very light whipped cream, coloured and flavoured so as to eat agreeably with it, and to please the eye as well: this may be tastefully garnished with preserved, or with fresh fruit; one of more recent invention, called the *Belgrave mould* (which is to be had of the originators, Mssrs. Temple and Reynolds, Princes Street, Cavendish Square, and also at 80 Motcomb Street, Belgrave Square), is of superior construction for the purpose, as it contains a large central cylinder and six smaller ones, which when withdrawn, after the jelly – which should be poured round, but not into them – is set, leave vacancies which can be filled either with jelly of another colour, or with fruit of different kinds (which must be secured in its place with *just liquid* jelly poured carefully in after it is arranged), or with blanc-mange, or any other isinglass-cream. The space occupied by the larger cylinder may be left empty, or filled, before the jelly is served with white or pale-tinted whipped cream. Water, only sufficiently warm to detach the jelly from them without heating or melting it, must be poured into the cylinders to *unfix* them; and to loosen the whole so as to unmould it easily, a cloth wrung out of very hot water must be wound round it, or the mould must be dipped quickly into some which is nearly or quite boiling. A dish should then be laid on it, it should be carefully reversed, and the mould lifted from it gently. It will sometimes require a slight sharp blow to detach it quite.

Eliza Acton *Modern Cookery for Private Families*

Swiss Cream or Trifle

Flavour pleasantly with lemon rind and cinnamon, a pint of rich cream, after having taken from it as much as will mix smoothly to a thin batter four teaspoonsful of the finest flour; sweeten it with six ounces of well-refined sugar in lumps; place it over a clear fire in a delicately clean saucepan, and when it boils stir in the flour, and simmer it for four or five minutes, stirring it gently without ceasing; then pour it out, and when it is quite cold

mix with it by degrees the strained juice of two moderate-sized and very fresh lemons. Take a quarter of a pound of macaroons, cover the bottom of a glass dish with a portion of them, pour in a part of the cream, lay the remainder of the macaroons upon it, add the rest of the cream, and ornament it with candied citron sliced thin. It should be made the day before it is wanted for table. The requisite flavour may be given to this dish by infusing in the cream the very thin rind of a lemon, and part of a stick of cinnamon slightly bruised, and then straining it before the flour is added; or these and the sugar may be boiled together with two or three spoonsful of water, to a strongly flavoured syrup, which, after having been passed through a muslin strainer, may be stirred into the cream... It may be flavoured with vanilla and maraschino, or with orange-blossoms at pleasure; but is *excellent* made as above.

Eliza Acton *Modern Cookery for Private Families*

Nesselrode pudding

We give Monsieur Careme's own receipt for this favourite and fashionable dish, not having ourselves had a good opportunity of proving it; but as it originated with him he is the best authority for it. It may be varied in many ways, which the taste of ingenuity of the reader will easily suggest. Boil forty fine sound Spanish chestnuts quite tender in plenty of water, take off the husks, and pound the chestnuts perfectly with a few spoonsful of syrup; rub them through a fine sieve, and mix them in a basin with a pint of syrup made with a pound of sugar clarified, and highly-flavoured with a pod of vanilla, a pint of rich cream, and the yolks of twelve eggs; thicken the mixture like a boiled custard; when it is cold put it into a freezing pot, adding a glass of maraschino, and make it set as an iced cream; then add an ounce of preserved citron cut in dice, two ounces of currants, and as many fine raisins stoned and divided (all of which should be soaked from the day before in some maraschino with a little sugar); the whole thus mingled, add a plateful of whipped cream, and the whites of three eggs prepared as for Italian meringue. When the pudding is perfectly frozen, mould it in a pewter mould of the form of a pine-apple, and place it again in the ice till wanted to serve. Preserved cherries may be substituted for the raisins and currants.

Eliza Acton *Modern Cookery for Private Families*

Brown bread ice cream

Mix 4 oz of stale brown breadcrumbs with ½ pint of whipped double cream and 3 oz of caster sugar flavoured with vanilla, and then put to freeze, as usual.

Major L *The Pytchley Book of Refined Cookery* 1886

Currant water ice

Pick a sufficiency of ripe currants from their stems, then squeeze the currants through a linen bag and to each quart of the juice allow a pound of powdered loaf sugar. Mix them together and when the juice is thoroughly melted put it into a freezer and freeze it in the manner of ice-cream. Serve it up in glass bowls.

J. H. Walsh *The Economical Housekeeper* 1857

Coffee ice cream

1½ oz of freshly-roasted and ground coffee
3 oz castor sugar
1 pint of custard
½ a gill of cream

Pour boiling water over the coffee, infuse for about ½ an hour, then strain, add the sugar, and let it cool. Make the custard according to the recipe, stir in the coffee; when cool, add the whipped cream and freeze.

Mrs Beeton *Family Cookery*

Ginger ice cream

1½ pints of custard
3 oz of preserved ginger
1 teaspoonful of ginger syrup

Make the custard. Cut the ginger into small dice, stir it with the syrup into the custard, and freeze.

Mrs Beeton *Family Cookery*

Lemon sorbet

8 lemons
2 oranges
8 oz of loaf sugar
2 oz of castor sugar
2 whites of eggs
3 pints of water

Place the loaf sugar in a stewpan with the 3 pints of water; let it dissolve, then boil and reduce it a little, and skim well during the process. Add the finely-grated rind of 2 lemons, the juice of the lemons and oranges, bring to the boil, strain, and let the preparation cool. Partially freeze, then add the well-whisked whites of eggs and the castor sugar, and continue the freezing until the desired consistency is obtained.

Mrs Beeton *Family Cookery*

Freezing ices

Mrs Beeton explained in detail how to freeze ice cream and sorbets in the days before ice cream making machines and electric freezers.

The materials usually employed for this purpose are ice and coarse salt, or freezing-salt, the correct proportions being 1 lb of salt to 8 or 10 lb of ice. More salt than this is often added with a view to making the mixture freeze more quickly, which it does for a short time, but the large proportion of salt causes the ice to melt speedily, and the freezing operation comes to a standstill unless the ice is frequently renewed. The ice tub or outer compartment of the machine must be filled with alternate layers of crushed ice and salt.

A good layer of ice at the bottom enables the freezing-pot to turn easily and more quickly than if it were placed on the bare wood.

Preparation of ices – The mixture to be frozen is placed in the freezing-pot or inner receptacle of the freezing machine, and the lid firmly secured. When the vessel has been quickly turned for a short time (some machines do not require to be turned), a thin coating of ice will have formed on the sides. This must be scraped down with the spatula, and well mixed with the liquid contents, and as soon as another layer has formed it must be dealt with in the same manner. This, and the turning, is continued until the mixture acquires a thick creamy consistency, when it is ready for moulding. To ensure success the following rules should be observed:

1 Avoid putting warm mixtures into the freezing-pot.
2 Add sweetening ingredients with discretion.
3 Avoid, as much as possible, the use of tin and copper utensils.
4 Carefully wipe the lid of the freezer before raising it, so as to prevent any salt getting into the mixture.

Moulding of ices – The ice, in the semi-solid condition in which it is taken from the freezing machine, is put into dry moulds, and well shaken and pressed down in the shape of them. If there is the least doubt about the lid fitting perfectly, it is better to seal the opening with a layer of lard, so as effectually to exclude the salt and ice. In any case the mould should be wrapped in 2 or 3 folds of kitchen paper when the freezing has to be completed with a pail. One part of salt should be added to 8 parts of ice and the quantity must be sufficient completely to surround the mould. It should be kept covered with ice and salt for 3 or 4 hours, when it will be ready to unmould. When a charge ice cave is available, the ice is simply moulded, placed in the cave, and kept there until sufficiently frozen.

Unmoulding ices – Ices should be kept in the moulds, buried in ice, until required. When ready to serve, remove the paper and the lard, when it has been used, dip the mould into cold water, and turn the ice on to a dish in the same way as jelly or cream.

Christmas with Dickens

Mamie Dickens wrote a series of reminiscent articles entitled 'My Father as I Recall Him' about Charles Dickens at home for *The Ladies Home Journal* in 1892. Here, she recalls a typical Christmas.

Christmas was always a time which in our home was looked forward to with eagerness and delight, and to my father it was a time dearer than any other part of the year I think. He loved Christmas for its deep significance as well as for its joys … Even in his most merry conceits of Christmas, there are always subtle and tender touches which will bring tears to the eyes, and make even the thoughtless have some special veneration for this most blessed anniversary.

In our childish days my father used to take us, every twenty-fourth day of December, to a toy shop in Holborn, where we were allowed to select our Christmas presents, and also any that we wished to give to our little companions. My father, although the most generous of mortals, did not observe, except in rare instances, the custom of sending Christmas gifts to people outside his home…

When we were only babies my father determined that we should be taught to dance, so as early as the Genoa days we were given our first lessons… Our progress in the graceful art delighted him, and his admiration of our success was evident when we exhibited to

A Merry Christmas with Lots of Things.

him … When 'the boys' came home for the holidays there were constant sieges of practice for the Christmas and New Year parties and more especially for the dance on Twelfth Night, the anniversary of my brother Charlie's birthday. Just before one of these celebrations my father insisted that my sister Katie and I should teach the polka step to him and Mr Leech. My father was much in earnest about learning to take that wonderful step correctly … Often he would practise gravely in a corner without either partner or music …

While I am writing of my father's fondness for dancing, a characteristic anecdote of him occurs to me. While he was courting my mother, he went one summer evening to call upon her. The Hogarths were living a little way out of London, in a residence which had a drawing-room opening with French windows on to a lawn. In this room my mother and her family were seated quietly after dinner on this particular evening, when suddenly a young sailor jumped through one of the open windows into the apartment, whistled and danced a hornpipe, and before they could recover from their amazement jumped out again. A few minutes later my father walked in at the door as sedately as though quite innocent of the prank and shook hands with everyone; but the sight of their amazed faces proving too much for his attempted sobriety, his hearty laugh was the signal for the rest of the party to join his merriment.

His dancing was at its best I think, in the 'Sir Roger de Coverly' – known in America, I am told as the 'Virginia Reel' – and in what are known as country dances… He was very fond of a country dance which he learned at the house of some dear friends at Rockingham Castle, which began with quite a stately minuet to the tune of 'God Save the Queen' and then dashed suddenly into 'Down the Middle and up Again'. His enjoyment of all our frolics was equally keen, and he writes to an American friend, apropos of one of our Christmas merry makings: 'Forster is out again, and if he don't go in again after the manner in which we have been keeping Christmas, he must be very strong indeed. Such dinings, such conjurings, such blindman's buffings, such theatre goings, such kissings out of old years and kissings in of new ones never took place in these parts before. To keep the Chuzzlewit going, and to do this little book, the carol, in

the odd times between two parts of it, was, as you may suppose pretty tight work. But when it was done I broke out like a madman, and if you could have seen me at a children's party at Macready's the other night going down a country dance with Mrs M. you would have thought I was a country gentleman of independent property residing on a tip-top farm, with the wind blowing straight in my face every day.'

At our holiday frolics he used sometimes to conjure for us, the equally noble art of the prestidigitator being among his accomplishments. He writes of this which he included in the list of our Twelfth Night amusements, to another American friend: 'The actuary of the national debt couldn't calculate the number of children who are coming here on Twelfth Night in honour of Charlie's birthday, for which occasion I have provided a magic lantern and divers other tremendous engines of that nature. But the best of it is that Forster and I have purchased between us the entire stock-in-trade of a conjuror, the practice and display whereof is entrusted to me. And if you could see me conjuring the company's watches into impossible tea-caddies and causing pieces of money to fly, and burning pocket handkerchiefs without burning 'em and practising in my own room without anybody to admire, you would never forget it as long as you live.'

But I think that our Christmas and New Year's tides at Gad's Hill were the happiest of all. Our house was always filled with guests, while a cottage in the village was reserved for the use of the bachelor members of our holiday party. My father, himself, always deserted work for the week, and that was almost our greatest treat. He was the fun and life of those gatherings, the true Christmas spirit of sweetness and hospitality filling his large and generous heart. Long walks with him were daily treats to be remembered. Games passed our evenings in jollity. 'Proverbs', a game of memory, was very popular, and it was one in which either my aunt or myself was apt to prove winner. Father's annoyance at our failure sometimes to lead was very amusing but quite genuine. Dumb Crambo was another favourite and one in which my father's great imitative ability showed finely. I remember one evening his dumb showing of the word 'frog' was so extremely laughable...

oDS Angel stooped
in bright array,
Fear not, he said,
but shout and sing!
To you in David's
town this day,
Is born a Saviour,
✦ Christ the King ✦

Our Christmas day dinners at Gad's Hill were particularly bright and cheery, some of our nearest neighbours joining our home party... The Christmas plum pudding had its own special dish of coloured repousse china, ornamented with holly. The pudding was placed on this with a sprig of real holly, lighted, and in this state placed in front of my father, its arrival being always the signal for applause. A prettily decorated table was his special pleasure and from my earliest girlhood the care of this devolved upon me. When I had everything in readiness, he would come with me to inspect the results of my labours, before dressing for dinner, and no word except of praise ever came to my ears.

He was a wonderfully neat and rapid carver, and I am happy to say taught me some of his skill in this. On Christmas Day we all had our glasses filled, and then my father, raising his, would say, 'Here's to us all. God bless us!' a toast which was rapidly and willingly drunk. One morning – it was the last day of the year I remember – while we were at breakfast at Gad's Hill, my father suggested that we should celebrate the evening by a charade to be acted in performance. The suggestion was received with acclamation, and amid shouts and laughing we were then and there, guests and members of the family, allotted our respected parts. My father went about collecting 'stage properties', rehearsals were called at least four times during the

morning, and in all our excitement no thought was given to that necessary part of a charade, the audience, whose business it is to guess the pantomime… Invitations were quickly dispatched to our neighbours, and additional preparations made for supper. In due time the audience came and the charade was acted so successfully that the evening stands out in my memory as one of the merriest and happiest of the many merry and happy evenings in our dear old home. My father was so extremely funny in his part that the rest of us found it almost impossible to maintain sufficient control over ourselves to enable the pantomime to proceed as it was planned to do. It wound up with a country dance, which had been invented that morning and practised quite a dozen times during the day, and which was concluded at just a few moments before midnight. Then leading us all, characters and audience, out into the wide hall, and throwing wide open the door, my father watch in hand, stood waiting to hear the bells ring in the New Year. All was hush and silence after the laughter and merriment! Suddenly the peal of bells sounded, and turning he said: 'A happy New Year to us all! God bless us.' Kisses, good wishes and shaking of hands brought us again back to the fun and gaiety of a few moments earlier. Supper was served; the hot mulled wine drunk in toasts, and the maddest and wildest of Sir Roger de Coverlys ended our evening and began our New Year.'

Chapter 7

Pantos and Boxes

There are a number of possible origins of the name 'Boxing Day'. Chambers traces it to the ancient Romans:

> 'who, at the season of the Saturnalia, practised universally the custom of giving and receiving presents. The fathers of the church denounced, on the ground of its pagan origin, the observance of such a usage by the Christians; but their anathemas had little practical effect and, in process of time, the custom of Christmas-boxes and New Year's gifts, like others adopted from the heathen, attained the position of a universally recognised institution. The

church herself has even got the credit of originating the practice of Christmas-boxes.

Other theories credit the Church with the idea in the first place, tracing it to the placing of alms boxes around each church during the approach to the Christmas season, the contents of which would be distributed to the poor on 26 December. Or from the practice of apprentices, servants and all sorts of workers asking their masters for small amounts of money – collected in little boxes that they broke open as soon as Christmas proper was finished – Boxing Day.

Chambers was well accustomed to the practice:

Christmas-boxes are still regularly expected by the postman, the lamplighter, the dustman, and generally by all those functionaries who render services to the public at large, without receiving payment therefore from any particular individual… St Stephen's Day, or the 26th of December, being the customary day for the claimants of Christmas-boxes going their rounds it has received popularly the designation of Boxing-day. In the evening, the new Christmas pantomime for the season is generally produced for the first time; and as the pockets of the working-classes, from the causes which we have above stated, have commonly received an extra supply of funds, the theatres are almost universally crowded to the ceiling on Boxing-night; whilst the 'gods' or upper gallery, exercise even more than their usual authority. In conclusion, we must not be too hard on Christmas-boxes… That many abuses did and still do cling to them, we readily admit; but there is also intermingled with them a spirit of kindliness and benevolence, which it would be very undesirable to extirpate.

Christmas boxes – another view

In 1849, *Punch* magazine took a rather less benevolent view than Chambers towards the giving of Christmas boxes:

> *The Christmas Box system is, in fact, a piece of horribly internecine strife between cooks and butchers' boys, lamp-lighters, beadles, and all classes of society, tugging at each other's pockets for the sake of what can be got under the pretext of seasonable benevolence. Our cooks bully our butchers for the annual box, and our butchers take it out of us in the course of the year by tacking false tails on to our saddles of mutton, adding false feet to our legs of lamb, and chousing us with large lumps of chump in our chops, for the purpose of adding to our bills by giving undue weight to our viands. Punch has resolved on the overthrow of the Boxing system, and down it will go before 1849 has expired.*

Needless to say, they did not succeed.

It's panto time!

The pantomime has a long and varied ancestry, though it became in Victorian times and remains to this day, uniquely English. It dates back to the medieval masque, a form of entertainment that was to reach its peak during the Elizabethan and Stuart eras. In the Eighteenth Century, the masque began to develop into something closer to the pantomime we would recognise today. Often they would have characters taken from the Italian *commedia dell'arte*, such as Harlequin, Scaramouche, Pantaloon and Columbine, or from classical legends. John Rich produced one such pantomime, *Harlequin Executed* at the Lincoln's Inn Fields Theatre in 1717 and this is generally credited as being the first English pantomime. His classical story was *Perseus and Andromeda* which he somehow wove in with the *commedia dell'arte* characters. As if this were not enough of a feat, he produced the first transformation scene.

Chambers was, on the whole, not impressed. 'Pantomimic acting,' he opines, 'had its place in the ancient drama, but the grotesque performances associated with our English Christmas, are peculiar to this country.' Cibber says that they originated in an attempt to make stage-

A Merry Christmas

dancing something more than motion without meaning. Rich seems to have grafted the scenic and mechanical features of the old masque upon the pantomimic ballet. Davies in his *Dramatic Miscellanies*, describes Rich's pantomimes as 'consisting of two parts – one serious, the other comic. By the help of gay scenes, fine habits, grand dances, appropriate music, and other decorations, he exhibited a story from Ovid's *Metamorphoses*, or some other mythological work. Between the pauses or acts of this serious representation, he interwove a comic fable, consisting chiefly of the courtship of Harlequin and Columbine, with a variety of surprising

adventures and tricks, which were produced by the magic wand of Harlequin; such as the sudden transformation of palaces and temples to huts and cottages; of men and women into wheel-barrows and joint-stools; of trees turned to houses; colonnades to beds of tulips; and mechanics shops into serpents and ostriches.'

Shortly before Victoria acceded to the throne, the pantomime was given an entirely new emphasis by one man, the clown Grimaldi. Born in London of Italian parents, he made his first appearance on

the stage of Sadlers Wells at the age of three. 'His genius,' says Chambers, 'elevated the Clown into the principal personage of the pantomime.'

The clown took over and the transformation scene became a permanent fixture of the panto, but the Victorians gradually lost all the earlier stock characters and replaced them with children's stories such as *Little Red Riding Hood* and *Cinderella*. The music hall, the Victorians' most popular form of theatre, also influenced the pantomime, so singing and other popular 'turns' from juggling to fire eating were all incorporated as part of the entertainment.

St Stephen

26 December is also St Stephen's Day. St Stephen was the first Christian martyr, stoned to death around 33AD, in honour of which he was given the first saint's day after Christmas. His life is well documented in the Acts

of the Apostles but he nevertheless seems to have been confused with a different St Stephen – a Ninth Century Swedish missionary who was a kind of patron saint for horses. This led in turn to the custom of bleeding horses on 26 December as a guarantee against disease for the coming year. In some places, the horse would then be given an especially generous meal. The practice had barely died out at the beginning of the Victorian era but the association with horses perhaps lingered in the tradition of the Boxing Day hunt.

WISHING YOU A VERY HAPPY CHRISTMAS.

Leftovers

The Victorians were true home economists – and the emphasis was on the economy. Waste was almost sinful, so not only was every part of an animal used in cooking or for other domestic purposes (such as tallow for candles), remnants from one meal would always be used up in another. So, after the day of the greatest feasting, Boxing Day was often a celebration of the leftovers. Mrs Beeton devotes an entire chapter to leftovers called:

The Art of 'Using Up' Cold Remains

'Dainty dishes which may be made with remains of cold meat, poultry, game, fish etc.'

> Great care should be taken that nothing which might, by proper management, be turned to good account, is thrown away, or suffered to be wasted in the kitchen. Most cooks like to work only with fresh materials, a practice which must be guarded against.
>
> *MEAT* – There are many ways of cutting up the remains of cold meat, and the manner in which this should be done depends entirely upon the nature of the dish to be made. Do not cut the meat into even slices, rather divide it into fancy shapes such as cutlets or fingers; it is thus more easily disguised, and the dish will be much more pleasing in appearance. Sometimes the slices must be thick, sometimes thin, and when curry is to be made the meat should be cut into dice. All the smaller scraps of meat, now left on the bones, must be carefully pared off and used up as mince. Bone, skin and gristle now alone remain, these should be chopped up very fine, well seasoned, covered with cold water and simmered down for stock.
>
> Reheat and serve the meat with suitable borders and garnishes in accordance with the instructions given in the various recipes. If the borders and garnishes are carefully prepared and arranged these uninteresting scraps of cold meat may be converted into most appetizing dishes. The cook should remember that in using up meat that has already been cooked, only steady, moderate heat is required; if too quickly cooked the meat will be rendered hard and tasteless.
>
> *BONES* – The shank bones of mutton, so little esteemed in

general, give richness to soups and gravies, if well soaked and bruised before they are added to the boiling liquor. Roast beef bones, or shank bones of ham, make excellent stock for soup.

CRUSTS may be dried in the oven and used for crumbling. Sippets for soup can be made by baking stale bread in the oven, and there are numerous puddings which have bread and crumbs as ingredients.

EGGS – When the whites of eggs are used for jelly, confectionery, or other purposes, a pudding or a custard should also be made, that the yolks may be used.

VEGETABLES – Cold vegetables may be used to garnish certain entrees; they may be employed in salads, soups, and hors d'oeuvres.

Beef curry

1¹/₂ lb of cold roast beef
1 pint of stock
1¹/₂ oz of butter or clarified dripping
1 tablespoonful of flour
1 tablespoonful of curry-powder
1 teaspoonful of curry-paste
1 sour apple
2 onions chopped
1 teaspoonful of lemon-juice
salt
4 oz rice

Put the bones and brown outside parts of the meat into a saucepan, cover with cold water, and boil for at least 2 hours, then strain and use. Cut the meat into slices about ¹/₂ an inch thick and 1 inch square. Melt the butter or dripping in a stewpan, fry the onions for a few minutes, then add the curry-powder and flour, and fry gently for about 5 minutes. Add the stock, curry-paste, sliced apple, and salt to taste, stir until the sauce boils and simmer gently for about ¹/₂ an hour. Now put in the meat, cover closely, draw the stewpan aside to prevent the contents boiling, and let it remain about ¹/₂ an hour for the meat to become impregnated with the flavour of the sauce. Arrange the meat in a pyramidal form in the centre of a hot dish, season the sauce to taste, add the lemon juice, and strain over the meat. Serve the rice separately.

Chicken rissoles

About 4 oz of cooked chicken
2 oz of cooked ham or tongue
4 button mushrooms
1 small truffle
$1/2$ an oz of butter
$1/2$ an oz of flour
$1/4$ of a pint of white stock
1 tablespoonful of cream or milk
salt and pepper to taste
egg
breadcrumbs
frying-fat
rough puff-paste

Chop the chicken and ham finely, cut the mushrooms and truffle into small dice. Melt the butter in a stewpan, stir in the flour, add the stock, stir and boil well. Put in the chicken and ham, season to taste, mix the ingredients well over the fire, then add the mushrooms, truffle and cream or milk, and put aside to cool. Roll out the paste as thinly as possible – stamp it out into round of about 2 inches diameter, pile a teaspoonful of the preparation in the centre, wet the edges with water, place another round of paste on the top, and press the edges together neatly. Brush over with egg and cover with breadcrumbs, and fry until lightly browned in hot fat. If preferred, half the quantity of the mixture may be enclosed in one round of paste, one half of which must be folded over to form them into half-moon shapes.

Time – About 1 $1/2$ hours.
Sufficient for 8 to 12 rissoles.

Cod hashe

2 lb of cooked cod
1¹/₂ oz of butter
1¹/₂ oz of flour
1 pint of milk
¹/₄ pint picked shrimps
pepper and salt
mashed potatoes
chopped parsley

Blend the butter and flour in a stewpan, and fry for a few minutes without allowing them to colour. Add the milk, and stir until boiling. Put in the cod, flaked into small pieces, and the shrimps. Cook these together until thoroughly hot, and season carefully. Make a deep border of mashed potatoes on a hot dish. Pour the hash in the centre, and sprinkle a little chopped parsley over the top.

Fish croquettes

¹/₂ a lb of cooked fish
¹/₄ of a lb of mashed potatoes
¹/₂ an oz of butter or good dripping
1 whole egg
breadcrumbs
milk
salt and pepper
frying-fat

Remove all skin and bone from the fish, then chop it coarsely. Heat the butter or dripping in a stewpan, add the fish, potatoes, season with salt and pepper to taste, and sufficient milk to moisten it thoroughly. Stir the preparation over the fire until well mixed, then turn it on to a plate. When cold, form it into cork-shaped pieces, brush over with beaten egg mixed with a little milk or water, coat with breadcrumbs, and fry in hot fat. Drain well, and serve garnished with crisply fried parsley.

Goose, hashed

Remains of roast goose
2 oz of butter or good dripping
1 oz of flour
1 pint of stock
2 finely chopped onions
6 button mushrooms
2 cloves
1 blade of mace
6 allspice
salt and pepper
croutons of fried bread
apple sauce

Cut the remains of the goose into neat pieces. Fry the onions in the butter or dripping, when turning brown add the flour, stir over the fire until it acquires a nut-brown colour, then add the stock, and boil for about 10 minutes. Add the goose, mushrooms, spices wrapped in muslin, and simmer very gently for about 3/4 of an hour. Arrange the pieces of goose neatly on a hot dish, remove the spices, season the sauce to taste, and pour it over. Garnish with croutons of fried bread, and serve with apple sauce.

Mutton réchauffé

Slices of cold mutton
1 onion finely chopped
a few slices of carrot
a few slices of turnip
^{3}/4 of a pint of stock made from bones and trimmings
1^1/2 oz of butter
1^1/2 oz of flour
1 tablespoonful of mushroom ketchup or some sharp sauce
salt and pepper

Simmer the bones, meat trimmings, turnip and carrot in just sufficient water to cover them for at least 1 hour, then strain and season to taste. Heat the butter, fry the onion until lightly browned, add the flour, stir and cook slowly until brown, and put in $^3/_4$ of a pint of stock. Stir until boiling, season to taste, add the mushroom ketchup, and boil gently for about 10 minutes. Place the slices of meat in the prepared sauce, let the stewpan stand for at least $^1/_2$ an hour, where the contents will remain just below simmering point, then arrange the meat on a hot dish, and strain the sauce over. Time – About 2 hours.

Shepherd's pie

$^1/_2$ a lb of cold mutton
1 lb of mashed potato
1 oz of butter or dripping
$^1/_2$ a pint of gravy or stock
1 teaspoonful of parboiled and finely-chopped onion
salt and pepper

Cut the meat into small thin slices. Melt $^1/_2$ the butter or fat in a stewpan, add to it the potato, salt and pepper, and stir over the fire until thoroughly mixed. Grease a pie-dish, line the bottom thinly with potato, put in the meat, sprinkle each layer with onions, salt and pepper, pour in the gravy, and cover with potato. The potato covering may be given a rough appearance by scoring it in every direction with a fork, or it may be made to resemble an ordinary crust by being smoothed over with a knife, notched at the edges, and brushed over with the yolk of egg before baking. Bake in a moderate oven until the surface is well browned.

Turkey, devilled

Cold roast turkey
Piquant or other suitable sauce
For the devilled butter:
1 oz of butter
$^1/_2$ a saltspoonful each of cayenne, black pepper and curry powder
a pinch of ground ginger

Mix the ingredients for the devilled butter together on a plate. Divide the turkey into pieces convenient for serving, remove all skin, score the flesh deeply, and spread lightly with the butter. Put aside, and let them remain for 1 hour, or longer when a highly seasoned dish is desired, then grill over the fire and serve with piquant or other suitable sauce.
Time – To grill, about 8 minutes.

Venison, hashed

Remains of roast venison: to each lb allow:
2 oz of butter
1¹/2 oz of flour
1/2 a glass of port wine (optional)
1 tablespoonful of red-currant jelly
gravy or stock

Cut the meat into neat slices, break up the bones, put them with the trimmings of the meat, and any venison gravy there may be, into a stewpan, cover with cold water, and simmer gently for about 1 hour. When water alone is used, a small onion and a bunch of herbs should be added. Melt the butter in a stewpan, stir in the flour, and fry until brown. Add the strained stock, stir until boiling, then put in the meat, wine (if used), jelly, salt and pepper to taste, cover the stewpan closely, and let it stand at the side of the stove for about 20 minutes for the meat to become thoroughly impregnated with the flavour of the sauce, which must not, however, be allowed to boil. Serve as hot as possible, garnished with croutons of fried or toasted bread, and hand red-currant jelly separately.

The Twelve Days of Christmas

The twelve days of Christmas last until 6 January so, though the excitement of Christmas Day itself was gone, Christmas was far from over.

The Church explains it thus: Advent, the weeks before Christmas, symbolises the coming of God to man; the Twelve Days of Christmas symbolise the coming of man to God, the last day, Epiphany being the day that the Magi, or Three Kings, arrived in Bethlehem, bringing gifts for the infant Jesus. The other twelve days have less significance than the first and last but they all are counted as part of the Christmas festival.

27 December – St John's Day

St John the Evangelist was 'the disciple whom Jesus loved' and, unlike many of the early Christians, he was not martyred but lived to the ripe old age of 94. His day was often associated with heavy drinking and Chambers explains the story thus:

> *A priest of Diana having denied the divine origin of the apostolic miracles challenged St. John to drink a cup of poison which he had prepared. The Evangelist, to remove his scepticism, after having first made on the vessel the sign of the cross, emptied it to the last drop without receiving the least injury. The purging of the cup from all evil is typified in the flight from it of Satan, the father of mischief, as represented in the medieval emblem. From this legend, a superstitious custom seems to have sprung of obtaining, on St. John's Day, supplies of hallowed wine, which was both drunk and used in the manufacture of manchets or little loaves; the individuals who partook of which were deemed secure from all danger of poison throughout the ensuing year. The subjoined allusion to the practice occurs in Googe's translation of Naogeorgus:*
> *'Nexte John the sonne of Zebedee hath his appoynted day,*
> *Who once by cruell Tyrannts' will, constrayned was they say*
> *Strong poyson up to drinke; therefore the Papistes doe beleeve*
> *That whoso puts their trust in him, no poyson them can greeve:*
> *The wine beside that halowed is in worship of his name,*
> *The Priestes doe give the people that bring money for the same.*

And after with, the selfe same wine are little manchets made
Agaynst the boystrous Winter stormes, and sundrie such like trade.
The men upon this solemne day, do take this holy wine
To make them strong, so do the maydes to make them faire and fine.'

28 December – Holy Innocents' Day or Childermas

Holy Innocents' Day takes its name from the slaughter by Herod of the children of Bethlehem in his attempt to murder the infant Jesus. It was traditionally the unluckiest day of the year and any project – especially a marriage or a new business venture – begun on 28 December was generally reckoned to be doomed to failure. It was a good day, though, for the Boy Bishops (see pages 33–4) who gave the sermon and took control of all the services.

29 December – St Thomas à Becket's Day

Thomas à Becket was murdered on 29 December 1170 by four of King Henry II's knights in response to the king asking, in a fit of rage, if no one would rid him of the turbulent priest causing him so many problems. Becket had been the king's chancellor and, indeed, his favourite courtier and friend. However, when the king suggested he become the next Archbishop of Canterbury, Becket resisted the idea – knowing that their relationship would have to change as he would have to serve his church before his king. Unfortunately, his king insisted. Becket soon became an ascetic monk rather than the king's boon companion and the two finally reached the nadir of their relationship when Becket was forced into exile because of his championing of the rights of the clergy to be tried in church rather than secular courts. Becket returned in 1170 and was murdered within the month. He was recognised as a martyr and canonised and Henry made a pilgrimage to his tomb in Canterbury and did penance there.

30 December – St Sabinus' Day

The 30 December marks the saints' days of a number of saints who are now (and indeed in Victorian times were) little known. They are St Sabinus, bishop of

Assisium, and his companions, martyred in 304; St Anysia, martyred in 304 and St Maximus, confessor, martyred about 662.

31 December – New Year's Eve

New Year's Eve or Hogmanay (see pages 143–57) as it is called in Scotland is also the saints' day of Saints Sylvester, Columba and Melania the Younger.

1 January – New Year's Day

New Year's Day (see pages 157–60) is also the saints' day of Saints Fulgentius, Almachus, Eugendus, Mochina, Odilo, Faine and Medina.

2 January – St Macarius' Day

St Macarius had the unlikely start in life of a confectioner in Alexandria in Egypt. He became, however, a hermit and such an extreme ascetic that he went down in the annals of self-denial and self-torment as one of the holiest anchorites. Chambers tells various stories about him:

> Hearing great things of the self-denial of the monks of Tabenna, he went there in disguise, and astonished them all by passing through Lent on the aliment furnished by a few green cabbage leaves eaten on Sundays. He it was, of whom the striking story is told, that, having once killed a gnat which bit him, he immediately hastened in a penitent and self-mortifying humour to the marshes of Scet'e, which abound with great flies, a torment even to the wild boar, and exposed himself to these ravaging insects for six months; at the end of which time his body was a mass of putrid sores, and he only could be recognised by his voice.

3 January – St Genevieve's Day

St Genevieve is the patron saint of Paris, dying on 3 January 512. She was born just outside the city in 422 and she entered a convent at the tender age of seven. At fifteen, she took the veil and was to acquire such a reputation for sanctity that she became a considerable influence on the rulers of the day, even over the Frank, Clovis, who was to govern Paris until both of their deaths.

4 January – St Titus' and St Gregory's Day

The 4 January is the day dedicated to St Titus (a disciple of St Paul), St Gregory, St Rigobert and St Ramon.

5 January – Old Christmas Eve

Before the calendar was reformed in 1582 by Pope Gregory, the old Julian Calendar (introduced by Julius Caesar) was universally used but it was based on 365 and a quarter days. It overestimated the length of the year by just over eleven minutes which, by the Sixteenth Century, meant the calendar was ten days out. The Gregorian Calendar was not adopted in England until 1751 by which time the English were eleven days out, celebrating Christmas on 6 January, so the 5th became known as Old Christmas Eve.

6 January – Twelfth Night

Twelfth Night, 6 January, known as Epiphany, marked the arrival of the Three Kings at the birthplace of Jesus and was the official ending of Christmas.

Chapter 8

Ring out the Old, Ring in the New

Whilst the inhabitants of South Britain are settling down again quietly to work after the festivities of the Christmas season, their fellow-subjects in the northern division of the island are only commencing their annual saturnalia, which, till recently, bore, in the licence and boisterous merriment which used to prevail, a most unmistakable resemblance to its ancient pagan namesake. The epithet of the Daft Days, applied to the season of the New Year in Scotland, indicates very expressively the uproarious joviality which characterised the period in question. This exuberance of joyousness – which, it must be admitted, sometimes led to great excesses – has now much declined, but New Year's Eve and New Year's Day constitute still the great national holiday in Scotland.

The celebrations may have calmed down slightly in Chambers' day compared to the wildness of the Eighteenth Century New Year's party but Scotland was still celebrating the turn of the year far more than Christmas. This was probably a result of the Reformation when the Scottish Protestants attacked the heathenish festivities of Christmas even more than the English did. But the Scots simply delayed the party for a week and turned the New Year into Hogmanay.

There is much speculation about the origins of the word 'Hogmanay'. One suggests it is derived from the Greek words for 'holy month' or 'holy moon'. Another takes the song beginning 'Hogmanay, Trollolay' to be a corruption of the French 'Homme est ne, trois rois la' ['man is born, three kings are there']. Then again, there is the ancient Scandinavian name 'Hoggu-nott' or 'Hogenat' for the night before the feast of Yule, the ancient Scandinavian feast of the winter solstice. Finally, there is the theory that it means 'to the mistletoe go' or 'to the mistletoe this New Year' from the French Touraine patois 'au gui menez' or 'au gui l'an neuf' respectively and both an allusion to the ancient Druidical practice of gathering mistletoe for the midwinter ceremonies.

Hogmanay also refers to the practice, still very much current in Victorian times, that involved, rather like gooding and wassailing, people asking for treats – in this case they were children and they were hoping for cheese and oatcakes. Chambers describes it thus:

> In country places in Scotland, and also in the more retired and primitive towns, it is still customary on the morning of the last day of the year, or Hogmanay, for the children of the poorer class of people to get themselves swaddled in a great sheet, doubled up in front, so as to form a vast pocket, and then to go along the streets in little bands, calling at the doors of the wealthier classes for an expected dole of oaten-bread. Each child gets one quadrant section of oat-cake (sometimes, in the case of particular favourites, improved by an addition of cheese), and this is called their hogmanay. In expectation of the large demands thus made upon them, the housewives busy themselves for several days before hand in preparing a suitable quantity of cakes. The children on coming to the door cry, 'Hogmanay!' which is in itself a sufficient announcement of their demands; but there are other exclamations which either are or might be used for the same purpose. One of these is:

'Hogmanay, Trollolay,
Give us of your white bread, and none of your gray.'

And another favourite rhyme is:
'Get up, goodwife, and shake your feathers,
And dinna think that we are beggars;
For we are bairns come out to play,
Get up and gie's our hogmanay.'

The following is of a moralising character, though a good deal of a truism:
'Get up, goodwife, and dinna sweir,
And deal your bread to them that's here;
For the time will come when ye'll be dead,
And then ye'll neither need ale nor bread.'

The most favourite of all, however, is more to the point than any of the foregoing:

'My feet's cauld, my shoon's thin;
Gie's my cakes, and let me rin!'

Guisers and guizards

All over Scotland, local celebrations to celebrate the end of the old year and the start of the new had their own particular charm. In Deerness, in Orkney, the town formed a huge band that went around the district, knocking at each door and singing. After singing, food and ale was shared with the band who would then go on to the next house. Hogmanay was the favourite time for the mummers (see page 44) to do their rounds in Scotland, though they also sometimes did them at Christmas, too. North of the border, however, they were known as 'guisers' or 'guizards' and they performed very similar plays to the mummers. Chambers was not overly impressed:

There is one rude and grotesque drama which they are

accustomed to perform... and which, in various fragments or versions, exists in every part of Lowland Scotland. The performers, who are never less than three, but sometimes as many as six, having dressed themselves, proceed in a band from house to house, generally contenting themselves with the kitchen for an arena; whither, in mansions presided over by the spirit of good humour, the whole family will resort to witness the spectacle.

The burning of the clavie

One of Scotland's most unusual ways of marking the turning of the year was in the burning of the clavie, as recorded in *The Banffshire Journal*.

Any Hogmanay afternoon, a small group of seamen and coopers, dressed in blue overfrocks, and followed by numbers of noisy youngsters, may be seen rapidly wending their way to the south-western extremity of the village, where it is customary to build the Clavie. One of the men bears on his shoulders a stout Archangel tar-barrel, kindly presented for the occasion by one of the merchants, who has very considerately left a quantity of the resinous fluid at the bottom. Another carries a common herring cask, while the remainder are laden with other raw materials, and the tools necessary for the construction of the Clavie. Arrived at the spot, three cheers being given for the success of the undertaking operations are commenced forthwith. In the first place, the tar-barrel is sawn into two unequal parts; the smaller forms the groundwork of the Clavie, the other is broken up for fuel.

A common fir prop, some four feet in length, called the 'spoke', being then procured, a hole is bored through the tub-like machine that, as we have already said is to form the basis of the unique structure, and a long nail, made for the purpose, and furnished gratuitously by the village blacksmith, unites the two. Curiously enough, no hammer is allowed to drive this nail, which is sent home by a smooth stone. The herring cask is next demolished, and the staves are soon undergoing a diminution at both extremities, in order to fit them for their proper position. They are nailed, at intervals of about two inches all round, to the lower edge of the Clavie barrel, while the other ends are firmly fastened to the spoke, an aperture being left sufficiently large to admit the head of a man. Amid tremendous cheering, the finished Clavie is now set up against the wall, which is mounted by two stout young men, who proceed to the business of filling and lighting.

A few pieces of the split-up tar-barrel are placed in a pyramidal form in the inside of the Clavie, enclosing a small space for the reception of a burning peat, when everything is ready. The tar, which had been previously removed to another vessel, is now poured over the wood; and the same inflammable substance is freely used, while the barrel is being closely packed with timber and other combustible materials, that rise twelve or thirteen inches above the rim.

By this time the shades of evening have begun to descend, and soon the subdued murmur of the crowd breaks forth into one loud, prolonged cheer, as the youth who was despatched for the fiery peat (for custom says no sulphurous Lucifer, no patent Congreve dare approach within the sacred precincts of the Clavie) arrives with his glowing charge. The master-builder relieving him of his precious trust, places it within the opening already noticed, where, revived by a hot blast from his powerful lungs, it ignites the surrounding wood and tar, which quickly bursts into a flame. During the short time the fire is allowed to gather strength, cheers are given in rapid succession for the Queen, the Laird, the Provost, the Town, the harbour and the Railway and then Clavie-bearer number one, popping his head between the staves is away with his flaming burden...

As fast as his heavy load will permit him, the bearer hurries along the well known route, followed by the shouting Burgheadians, the boiling tar meanwhile trickling down in dark sluggish streams all over his back. Nor is the danger of scalding the only one he who essays to carry the Clavie has to confront, since the least stumble is sufficient to destroy his equilibrium. Indeed, this untoward event, at one time looked on as a dire calamity, foretelling disaster to the place, and certain death to the bearer in the course of next year, not infrequently occurs. Having reached the junction of two streets, the carrier of the Clavie is relieved; and while the change is being effected, firebrands plucked from the barrel are thrown among the crowd, who eagerly scramble for the tarry treasure, the possession of which was of old deemed a sure safeguard against all unlucky contingencies.

Again the multitude bound along; again they halt for a moment as another individual takes his place as bearer – a post for the honour of which there is sometimes no little striving. The circuit of the town being at length completed, the Clavie is borne along the principal street to a small hill near the northern extremity of the promontory called the 'Doorie', on the summit of which a freestone pillar, very much resembling an ancient altar, has been built for its reception, the spoke fitting into a socket in the centre. Being now firmly seated on its throne, fresh fuel is heaped on the Clavie, while, to make the fire burn the brighter, a barrel with the ends knocked out is placed on the top. Cheer after cheer rises from the crowd below, as the efforts made to increase the blaze are crowned with success.

Though formerly allowed to remain on the Doorie the whole night, the Clavie is now removed when it has burned about half an hour. Then comes the most exciting scene of all. The barrel is lifted from the socket, and thrown down on the western slope of the hill, which appears to be all in one mass of flame—a state of matters that does not, however, prevent a rush to the spot in search of embers. Two stout men, instantly seizing the fallen Clavie, attempt to demolish it by dashing it to the ground: which is no sooner accomplished than a final charge is made among the blazing fragments, that are snatched up in total, in spite of all the powers of combustion, in an incredibly short space of time.

Up to the present moment, the origin of this peculiar custom is involved in the deepest obscurity. Some would have us to believe that we owe its introduction to the Romans; and that the name Clavie is derived from the Latin word clavus, a nail — witches being frequently put to death in a barrel stuck full of iron spikes; or from clavis, a key — the rite being instituted when Agricola discovered that Ptoroton, i.e., Burghead, afforded the grand military key to the north of Scotland.

As well might these wild speculators have remarked that Doorie, which may be spelled Durie, sprang from durus, cruel, on account of the bloody ceremony celebrated on its summit. Another opinion has been boldly advanced by one party, to the effect that the Clavie is Scandinavian in origin, being introduced by the Norwegian Vikings, during the short time they held the promontory in the beginning of the eleventh century, though the theorist advances nothing to prove his assumption, save a quotation from Scott's Marmion; while, to crown all, we have to listen to a story that bears on its face its own condemnation, invented to confirm the belief that a certain witch, yclept, a Kitty Clavers, bequeathed her name to the singular rite.

Unfortunately, all external evidence being lost, we are compelled to rely entirely on the internal, which we have little hesitation, however, in saying points in an unmistakable manner down through the long vistas of our national history to where the mists of obscurity *hang around the Druid worship of our forefathers. It is well known that the elements of fire were often present in Druidical orgies and customs (as witness their cran-tara); while it is universally admitted that the bonfires of May-day and Mid-summer eve, still kept up in different parts of the country, are vestiges of these rites. And why should not the Clavie be so too, seeing that it bears throughout the stamp of a like parentage? The carrying home of the embers, as a protection from the ills of life, as well as other parts of the ceremony, finds a counterpart in the customs of the Druids; and though the time of observance be somewhat different, yet may not the same causes (now unknown ones) that have so greatly modified the Clavie have likewise operated in altering the date, which, after all, occurs at the most solemn part of the Druidical year?*

The burning of tar barrels and bonfires and the lights of torches from them were common New Year's practices. One other that was certainly current in Victorian times – and is indeed extant today – is Up-Helly-Aa, Norse for 'end of the holiday'. The holiday in this case was the Viking Yule, or midwinter festival and it took place on the Shetland Isles. In keeping with the old Yule, it took place towards the end of January and, instead of a barrel or a bonfire, the islanders burned an old fishing boat instead.

First footing

Says Chambers, in reflective mood:

The close of the year, brings along with it a mingled feeling of gladness and melancholy – of gladness in the anticipation of brighter days to come with the advent of the New Year, and of melancholy in reflections on the fleeting nature of time, and the gradual approach to the inevitable goal in the race of life. That so interesting an occasion should be distinguished by some observance or ceremony appears but natural, and we accordingly find various customs prevail, some sportive, others serious, and others in which both the mirthful and pensive moods are intermingled.

One of the best known and most general of these customs is, that of sitting up till twelve o'clock on the night of the 31st December, and, then, when the eventful hour has struck, proceeding to the house-door, and unbarring it with great formality to 'let out the Old, and let in the New Year.' The evening in question is a favourite occasion for social gatherings in Scotland and the north of England, the assembled friends thus welcoming together the birth of another of Father Time's ever-increasing, though short-lived progeny. In Philadelphia, in North America, we are informed that the Old Year is there 'fired out,' and the New Year 'fired in,' by a discharge of every description of firearm—musket, fowling-piece, and pistol. In the island of Guernsey, it used to be the practice of children to dress up a figure in the shape of a man, and after parading it through the parish, to bury it on the sea-shore, or in some retired spot. This ceremony was styled 'enterrer le vieux bout de l'an'.

A custom prevails, more especially among English dissenters, of having a midnight service in the various places of worship on the last night of the year, the occasion being deemed peculiarly adapted both for pious meditations and thankfulness, and also for the reception and retention of religious impressions. And to the community at large, the passing away of the Old Year and the arrival of his successor is heralded by the peals of bells, which, after twelve o'clock has struck, burst forth from every steeple, warning us that another year has commenced. At such a moment, painful reflections will obtrude themselves, of time misspent and opportunities neglected, of the fleeting nature of human existence and enjoyment, and that ere many more years have elapsed, our joys and sorrows, our hopes and our forebodings, will all, along with ourselves, have become things of the past.

While Chambers describes a remarkably low key English midnight, in Scotland the twelve strikes of the clock were the signal that the celebrations were about to begin. While the bells were ringing, all the doors

– and sometimes the windows – were opened to let the old year out and the new year in. Just in case there were any old spirits or influences left the family could join in with the noise, banging trays and pots and ringing bells. The house would have been cleaned until it was spotless, debts would have been paid, the beds made up with clean sheets, anything that was borrowed returned and all unfinished business, of whatever description, finished. Now was the moment that the new year could start with a clean slate and it would be welcomed over the threshold in the form of the first footer.

The first footer – literally the first person to step into the house – would bring with him a small branch and a bunch of mistletoe. He would lay the branch on the fire, kiss all the women and shake the hands of all the men. Alternatively, he could bring bread, salt and coal, placing the first two on the table (to ensure plenty for the coming year) and the coal on the fire and, again, shake the hands of all the men and kiss all the women. He would then stay and enjoy the party if he was not going first-footing elsewhere. To be welcomed as first footer – and it was generally the warmest of welcomes – you had to conform to a very particular type. Firstly, you had to be male and, secondly, red haired (though in some places dark haired). Anyone with unusual characteristics – flat feet, a squint, lameness, or eyebrows that met in the middle – was considered bad luck, as were all women. However, if you were the right first footer, everyone could heave a sigh of relief and enjoy the party. The traditional drink was 'het ale' and besides the usual feast, oatcakes, cheese, shortbreads and typically Scottish cakes were eaten. No one would go to bed until long after midnight and the streets would be full for hours – one traveller remarked that the streets of Edinburgh were busier at midnight than at midday.

Het [hot] ale

1 quart of good ale
1 glass of rum or brandy
1 tablespoonful of castor sugar
a pinch of ground cloves

a pinch of grated nutmeg
a good pinch ground ginger

Put the ale, sugar, cloves, nutmeg, and ginger into an ale-warmer or stewpan, and bring nearly to boiling point. Add the brandy and more sugar and flavouring if necessary and serve at once.

Haggis

A sheep's paunch (stomach) and pluck (heart, liver and lungs)
1 lb of finely chopped beef suet
$1/2$ a pint of oatmeal
2 finely chopped Spanish onions
2 tablespoonfuls of salt
1 teaspoonful of pepper
$1/2$ a nutmeg finely grated
$1^1/2$ pints of good stock or gravy
the juice of 1 lemon

Soak the paunch for several hours in salt and water, then turn it inside out, and wash it thoroughly in several waters. Wash the pluck, cover the liver with cold water, boil it for about $1^1/2$ hours, and at the end of $3/4$ of an hour, add to it the heart and lights (lungs). Chop half the liver coarsely and the rest with the heart and lights finely, mix all together, add the oatmeal, suet, onions, salt, pepper, nutmeg, lemon juice and stock. Turn these ingredients into the paunch, sew up the opening, taking care that sufficient space is left for the oatmeal to swell: if the paunch be over full, there is a possibility of its bursting. Put the haggis into boiling water, and cook gently for about 3 hours; during the first hour it should be occasionally pricked with a needle, to allow the air to escape. As a rule, neither sauce nor gravy is served with a haggis.

Mrs Beeton *Family Cookery*

Neeps

8 large carrots
8 turnips
$^1/_2$ teaspoonful nutmeg
$^1/_2$ pint of single cream
salt and pepper to taste

Peel the turnips, scrub the carrots
and remove the tops. Chop both
into rough quarters and boil in
salted water for 20 minutes. Remove
from the water and mash thoroughly with the
remaining ingredients.

Scotch shortbread

2 lb of flour
$^1/_4$ of a lb of cornflour or ground rice
1 lb of butter
$^1/_4$ of a lb of castor sugar
1 oz of sweet almonds
a few strips of candied orange-peel

Beat the butter to a cream, add gradually the flour,
sugar and sweet almonds, blanched and
shredded. Knead until it is quite smooth,
divide into 6 pieces and place each
cake on a separate piece of paper,
roll out square to the thickness of
1 inch, and pinch round the edges.
Prick well with a skewer,
ornament with 1 or 2 strips of
candied orange-peel, and bake in
a moderately hot oven from 25 to
30 minutes.

Mrs Beeton *Family Cookery*

Scotch oatcakes

¹/₂ a lb of double-dressed Scotch oatmeal
¹/₂ an oz of fat or butter
1 good pinch of bicarbonate of soda

Put about ¹/₂ a lb of meal into a 1-pint basin and have a teacup into which put a small piece of butter or lard, the size of a small hazel-nut, and a pinch of bicarbonate of soda: pour on this about ¹/₂ a teacup of hot water, stir until the butter is melted and soda is dissolved, then mix quickly with the meal in the basin with the point of a knife, and when the mixture is thoroughly stirred turn it out on to a paste board, and mould it quite compactly, keeping it round and flat, and with the knuckles spreading it gradually, taking care that it does not crack at the edges; strew plenty of dry meal over it to roll it out with the crimped roller, and every now and then rub the surface with the flat of the hand to disengage all superfluous meal; when rolled as thin as a penny-piece, and fairly round, put the knife in the centre and divide it into three, then, having the griddle over the fire, lay the cakes on the hot iron, the plain side down, and as the cakes get done move them in succession from a cool spot to a hotter. By pressing the nail on the surface, if they are not doughy it is a sign that they are sufficiently baked. With care the cakes can be baked in a greased frying-pan with a trivet underneath. Now move them from over the fire on to the toaster before the fire, and watch that they dry gradually, for they will soon burn, and as they are taken from the fire stand them carefully on edge till they are quite cold. While this is proceeding over the fire mix more cakes, and when one is ready to go to the toaster, fill up the vacant place. About 10 minutes to bake.

Mrs Beeton *Family Cookery*

Dundee cake

12 oz butter
12 oz white sugar
6 eggs
1 lb flour
1 teaspoonful of baking-powder
12 oz currants
6 oz stoned and chopped raisins
8 oz sultanas
4 oz chopped mixed peel
grated rind of $1/2$ lemon
$3/4$ teaspoonful ground cinnamon
$1/4$ teaspoonful grated nutmeg
a little milk if necessary
$1/2$ gill brandy
$1/4$ lb almonds

Cream the butter and sugar together in a basin, add the well-beaten eggs one at a time, and brandy, stir quickly. Mix in the sieved flour and baking powder, cleaned fruit, the almonds peeled and chopped and lemon rind. If necessary add a little milk, but the mixture must not be too moist. Place the cake mixture in a prepared tin, sprinkle over the remainder of the almonds, and bake it in a moderate oven for about 2-$2^1/2$ hours. When cooked and firm to the touch place the cake on a wire sieve or rack to cool.

Mrs Beeton *Family Cookery*

Ankersocks

Ankersocks are gingerbread loaves – this recipe is Eliza Acton's and instead of her 'shallow square tin pan' a loaf tin could be used instead.

Whisk four strained or well-cleared eggs to the lightest possible froth and pour to them, by degrees, a pound and a quarter of treacle, still beating them lightly. Add, in the same manner, six ounces of pale brown sugar free from lumps, one pound of sifted flour, and six ounces of good butter, just sufficiently warmed to be liquid, and no more, for if hot, it would render the cake heavy; it should be poured in small portions to the mixture, which should be well beaten up with the back of a wooden spoon as each portion is thrown in: the success of the cake depends almost entirely on this part of the process. When properly mingled with the mass, the butter will not be perceptible on the surface and if the cake be kept light by constant whisking, large bubbles will appear in it to the last. When it is so far ready, add to it one ounce of Jamaica ginger and a large teaspoonful of cloves in fine powder, with the lightly grated rinds of two fresh full-sized lemons. Butter thickly, in every part, a shallow square tin pan, and bake the gingerbread slowly for nearly or quite an hour in a gentle oven.

New Year presents

There was a custom of giving presents to friends and family on New Year's Day that dated back to the Romans. By the time of the Victorians, though, it had become limited in England at least to gifts made by parents to their children. In France, however, it was still as popular as ever. Chambers quotes from the journal of an Englishman who experienced the Parisian New Year:

> *Carriages, says this writer, may be seen rolling through the streets with cargoes of bon-bons, souvenirs, and the variety of etceteras with which little children and grown up children are bribed into good humour; and here and there pastrycooks are to be met with, carrying upon boards enormous temples, pagodas, churches, and playhouses, made of fine flour and sugar, and the embellishments which render French pastry so inviting. But there is one street in Paris to which a New-Year's Day is a whole year's fortune – this is the Rue des*

Lombards, where the wholesale confectioners reside; for in Paris every trade and profession has its peculiar quarter. For several days preceding the 1st of January, this street is completely blocked up by carts and wagons laden with cases of sweetmeats for the provinces. These are of every form and description which the most singular fancy could imagine; bunches of carrots, green peas, boots and shoes, lobsters and crabs, hats, books, musical instruments, gridirons, frying-pans, and sauce-pans; all made of sugar, and coloured to imitate reality, and all made with a hollow within to hold the bon-bons.

The most prevailing device is what is called a cornet; that is, a little cone ornamented in different ways, with a bag to draw over the large end, and close it up. In these things, the prices of which vary from one franc (tenpence) to fifty, the bon-bons are presented by those who choose, to be at the expense of them, and by those who do not, they are only wrapped in a piece of paper; but bon-bons, in some way or other, must be presented. It would not, perhaps, be an exaggeration to state that the amount expended for presents on New-Year's Day in Paris, for sweet-meats alone, exceeds 500,000 francs, or £20,000 sterling. Jewellery is also sold to a very large amount, and the fancy articles exported in the first week of the year to England and other countries, is computed at one-fourth of the sale during the twelvemonths. In Paris, it is by no means uncommon for a man of 8000 or 10,000 francs a year, to make presents on New-Year's Day which cost him a fifteenth part of his income. No person able to give must on this day pay a visit empty-handed.

Everybody accepts, and every man gives according to the means which he possesses. Females alone are excepted from the charge of giving. A pretty woman, respectably connected, may reckon her New-Year's presents at something considerable. Gowns, jewellery, gloves, stockings, and artificial flowers fill her drawing-room: for in Paris it is a custom to display all the gifts, in order to excite emulation, and to obtain as much as possible. At the palace, the New-Year's Day is a complete jour de fête. Every branch of the royal family is then expected to make handsome presents to the king. For the six months preceding January 1824, the female branches were busily occupied in preparing presents of their own manufacture, which would fill at least two common-sized wagons.

The Duchess de Berri painted an entire room of japanned panels, to be set up in the palace, and the Duchess of Orleans prepared an elegant screen. An English gentleman, who was admitted suddenly

into the presence of the Duchess de Berri two months before, found her and three of her maids of honour, lying on the carpet, painting the legs of a set of chairs, which were intended for the king. The day commences with the Parisians, at an early hour, by the interchange of their visits and bon-bons. The nearest relations are visited first, until the furthest in blood have had their calls; then friends and acquaintances. The conflict to anticipate each other's calls, occasions the most agreeable and whimsical scenes among these proficients in polite attentions. In these visits, and in gossiping at the confectioners' shops, which are the great lounge for the occasion, the morning of New-Year's Day is passed; a dinner is given by some member of the family to all the rest, and the evening concludes, like Christmas Day, with cards, dancing, or any other amusement that may be preferred.

Chapter 9

Wise Men and Feasts of Fools

Twelfth Night marks both the end of the Christmas celebrations and the day of the Epiphany, the coming of the Magi to Bethlehem to bring their presents of gold, frankincense and myrrh to the infant Jesus. Epiphany comes from a Greek word, meaning 'appearance', signifying the manifestation of Christ to mankind in the form of the three Magi or Wise Men. Melchior brought gold to symbolise his royalty as the promised King of the Jews; Jasper brought frankincense, in token of his divinity and Balthazar brought myrrh, symbolising the sorrows of his human condition and eventual sacrifice.

Twelfth Night was to become an enormously popular festival. One of its most enduring manifestations was in the Twelfth Night Cake. A large cake was baked with a bean inserted and whoever was cut the piece that had the bean became Twelfth Night King. A pea could also be put in the cake and this would designate the Queen for the day. If a woman found the bean, she could choose her king and if a man found the pea he could choose the queen. Chambers points out that the festival was marked equally in Europe:

> *The importance of this ceremony in France, where the mock sovereign is named* Le Roi de la Fève, *is indicated by the proverbial phrase for good luck,* Il a trouvé la fève au gâteau *(he has found the bean in the cake). In Rome, they do not draw king and queen as in England, but indulge in a number of jocularities, very much for the amusement of children. Fruit-stalls and confectioners' shops are dressed up with great gaiety. A ridiculous figure, called Beffana, parades the streets, amidst*

a storm of popular wit and nonsense. The children, on going to bed, hang up a stocking, which the Beffana is found next morning to have filled with cakes and sweetmeats if they have been good, but with stones and dirt if they have been naughty.

The Victorians visited the confectioners' shops to buy their Twelfth Cakes which ranged in a price from a few shillings to several guineas, the most extravagant being made in the shapes of ships and forts, complete with sentinels and flags. They took up the idea, begun in the previous century, of having not just a king and queen but an entire court and packs of Twelfth Night cards were sold, representing ministers, maids of honour, and other attendants. The card you picked would give you your character for the rest of the night. John Britton, in his autobiography, recalls he 'suggested and wrote a series of Twelfth-Night Characters, to be printed on cards, placed in a bag, and drawn out at parties on the memorable and merry evening of that ancient festival. They were sold in small packets to pastry cooks, and led the way to a custom which annually grew to an extensive trade. For the second year, my pen-and-ink characters were accompanied by prints of the different personages by Cruikshank (father of the inimitable George), all of a comic or ludicrous kind.' These Twelfth Night celebrations were probably the last remnant of the much more raucous entertainments that belonged to the court of the Lord of Misrule, a medieval custom that had much in common with the election of boy bishops to run cathedrals and the

French Feast of Fools. The Twelve Days of Christmas (though the feast could sometimes run on for even longer) were a time when the 'natural order' was reversed. The servant could become the master, the clown or jester could become the lord. He would then 'reign' over a period of revels in which most of the normal rules that governed society could be overturned without any threat of retribution.

According to Chambers:

> In the university of Cambridge, the functions of the Lord of Misrule were performed by one of the Masters of Arts, who was regularly elected to superintend the annual representation of Latin plays by the students, besides taking a general charge of their games and diversions during the Christmas season, and was styled the Imperator or Praefectus Ludorum. A similar Master of Revels was chosen at Oxford. But it seems to have been in the Inns of Court in London that the Lord of Misrule reigned with the greatest splendour, being surrounded with all the parade and ceremony of royalty, having his lord-keeper and treasurer, his guard of honour, and even his two chaplains, who preached before him on Sunday in the Temple Church. On Twelfth Day, he abdicated his sovereignty, and we are informed that in the year 1635, this mock-representative of royalty expended in the exercise of his office about two thousand pounds from his own purse, and at the conclusion of his reign was knighted by Charles I at Whitehall. The office, indeed, seems to have been regarded among the Templars as a highly-honourable one, and to have been generally conferred on young gentlemen of good family.

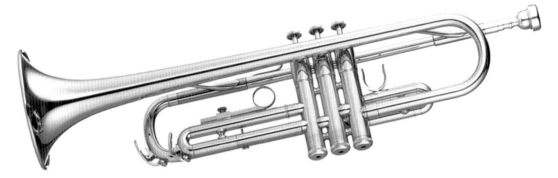

The following is an extract from the 'articles' drawn up by the Right Worshipful Richard Evelyn, Esq, father of the author of the Diary, and deputy-lieutenant of the counties of Surrey and Sussex, for appointing and defining the functions of a Christmas Lord of Misrule over his estate at Wotton: 'Imprimis, I give free leave to Owen Flood, my trumpeter, gentleman, to be Lord of Misrule of all good orders during the twelve days. And also, I give free leave to the said Owen Flood to command all and every person or persons whatsoever, as well servants as others, to be at his command whensoever he shall sound his trumpet or music, and to do him good service, as though I were present myself, at their perils I give full power and authority to his lordship to

A happy Christmas to you

New Year Wishes

break up all locks, bolts, bars, doors, and latches, and to fling up all doors out of hinges, to come at those who presume to disobey his lordship's commands. God save the King!'

We are informed that a favourite mode for his lordship to enter on the duties of his office was by explaining to the company that he absolved them of all their wisdom, and that they were to be just wise enough to make fools of themselves. No one was to sit apart in pride or self-sufficiency, to laugh at others. Moreover, he (the Lord of Misrule) came endowed with a magic power to turn all his auditory into children, and that, while his sovereignty lasted, he should take care that they conducted themselves as such. So fealty was sworn to the 'merry monarch', and the reign of fun and folly forthwith commenced. In the pantomime of the present day, we see in the mischievous pranks of the Clown, who parodies all the ordinary occupations of grave and serious life, a reproduction under a modern form of the extravagances of the Lord of Misrule.

There can be no doubt that scandalous abuses often resulted from the exuberant licence assumed by the Lord of Misrule and his satellites. It need, therefore, occasion no surprise to find their proceedings denounced in no measured terms by Prynne and other zealous Puritans. 'If,' says the author of the Histrio-Mastix, 'we compare our Bacchanalian Christmasses and New-year's Tides with these Saturnalia and Feasts of Janus, we shall find such near affinitye betweene them both in regard of time (they being both in the end of December and on the first of January) and in their manner of solemnising (both of them being spent in revelling, epicurisme, wantonesse, idlenesse, dancing, drinking, stage-plaies, masques, and carnall pompe and jollity), that we must needes conclude the one to be but the very ape or issue of the other. Hence Polydore Virgil affirmes in express tearmes that our Christmas Lords of Misrule (which custom, saith he, is chiefly observed in England), together with dancing, masques, mummeries, stageplayes, and such other Christmass disorders now in use with Christians, were derived from these Roman Saturnalia and Bacchanalian festivals; which (concludes he) should cause all pious Christians eternally to abominate them.'

Twelfth Cake

A Twelfth Cake, or any important cake, if made at home, will require care, attention and good materials. If these are given, and the following recipe attended to, the result can scarcely fail to be satisfactory, and a considerable saving may be effected, compared with what the same cake would have cost if bought at a confectioner's. Before beginning to mix the cake all the ingredients would be prepared, the flour dried and sifted, the currants washed, dried and picked, the nutmegs grated, the spices pounded, the candied fruit cut into thin slices, the almonds bruised with orange-flower or rose water, but not to a paste, the sugar sifted, and the eggs thoroughly whisked, yolks and whites separately. Care should be taken to make the cake and to keep the fruit in a warm place and, unless the weather is very warm, to whisk the eggs in a pan set in another containing hot water. To make the cake, put two pounds of fresh butter into a large bowl, then add two pounds of powdered sugar, a large nutmeg grated, and a quarter of an ounce each of powdered cinnamon, powdered mace, powdered ginger and powdered allspice. Beat the mixture for ten minutes, add gradually twenty eggs, and beat the cake for

twenty minutes. Work in two pounds of flour, four pounds of currants, half a pound of bruised almonds, half a pound of candied citron and last of all a claret glassful of brandy and beat the cake lightly. Into a cake tin with doubled paper well buttered, pour in the mixture, and be careful that it does no more than three-parts fill it, that there may be room for the cake to rise. Cover the top with paper, set the tin on an inverted plate in the oven to keep it from burning at the bottom and bake in a slow but well-heated oven. When it is nearly cold, cover it as smoothly as possible with sugar icing three quarters of an inch thick. Ornament with fancy articles of any kind, with a high ornament in the centre; these may frequently be hired of the confectioner. In order to ascertain whether the cake is done enough, plunge a bright knife into the centre of it, and if it comes out bright and clear the cake is done. A cake of this description will, if properly made, and kept in a cool dry place, keep for twelve months. If cut too soon it will crumble and fall into pieces. It will be at its best when it has been kept for four months.

Cassell's *Dictionary of Cookery*, 1874

Twelfth Day Eve

The day before Twelfth Night was associated with the fertility of animals and crops and there were still plenty of what Chambers describes as 'rustic festivals' in England during Victoria's reign:

> In Herefordshire, at the approach of the evening, the farmers with their friends and servants meet together, and about six o'clock walk out to a field where wheat is growing. In the highest part of the ground, twelve small fires, and one large one, are lighted up. The attendants, headed by the master of the family, pledge the company in old cider, which circulates freely on these occasions. A circle is formed round the large fire, when a general shout and hallooing takes place, which you hear answered from all the adjacent villages and fields. Sometimes fifty or sixty of these fires may be all seen at once. This being finished, the company return home, where the good housewife and her maids are preparing a good supper. A large cake is always provided, with a hole in the middle. After supper, the

company all attend the bailiff (or head of the oxen) to the wain-house, where the following particulars are observed: The master, at the head of his friends, fills the cup (generally of strong ale), and stands opposite the first or finest of the oxen. He then pledges him in a curious toast: the company follow his example, with all the other oxen, and addressing each by his name. This being finished, the large cake is produced and, with much ceremony, put on the horn of the first ox, through the hole above mentioned. The ox is then tickled, to make him toss his head: if he throw the cake behind, then it is the mistress's perquisite; if before (in what is termed the boosy), the bailiff himself claims the prize. The company then return to the house, the doors of which they find locked, nor will they be opened till some joyous songs are sung. On their gaining admittance, a scene of mirth and jollity ensues, which lasts the greatest part of the night.

The custom is called in Herefordshire 'Wassailing'. The fires are designed to represent the Saviour and his apostles, and it was customary as to one of them, held as representing Judas Iscariot, to allow it to burn a while, and then put it out and kick about the materials.

At Pauntley, in Gloucestershire, the custom has in view the prevention of the smut in wheat. All the servants of every farmer assemble in one of the fields that has been sown with wheat. At the end of twelve lands, they make twelve fires in a row with straw; around one of which, made larger than the rest, they drink a cheerful glass of cider to their master's health, and success to the future harvest; then returning home, they feast on cakes made with carraways, soaked in cider, which they claim as a reward for their past labour in sowing the grain.

In the south hams [villages] of Devonshire, on the eve of the Epiphany, the farmer,

attended by his workmen, with a large pitcher of cider, goes to the orchard, and there encircling one of the best bearing trees, they drink the following toast three several times:

Here's to thee, old apple-tree,
Whence thou mayst bud,
and whence thou mayst blow!
And whence thou mayst bear apples enow!
Hats full! Caps full!
Bushel—bushel—sacks full,
And my pockets full too! Huzza!

This done, they return to the house, the doors of which they are sure to find bolted by the females, who, be the weather what it may, are inexorable to all entreaties to open them till some one has guessed at what is on the spit, which is generally some nice little thing, difficult to be hit on, and is the reward of him who first names it. The doors are then thrown open, and the lucky clod-pole receives the tit-bit as his recompense. Some are so superstitious as to believe, that if they neglect this custom, the trees will bear no apples that year.

Dickens' Twelfth Night

Mamie Dickens wrote of her recollections of the Dickens' family – and, above all of her father – celebrating Twelfth Night in 'My Father as I Recall Him' in the *Ladies' Home Journal* in 1892:

> *My father was again in his element at the Twelfth Night parties … For many consecutive years, Miss Coutts, now the Baroness Burdett Coutts, was in the habit of sending my brother, on this his birthday anniversary, the most gorgeous of Twelfth-cakes, with an accompanying box of bonbons and Twelfth Night characters. The cake was cut, and the favours and bonbons distributed at the birthday supper, and it was then that my father's kindly, genial nature overflowed in merriment. He would have something droll to say to every one, and under his attentions the shyest child would brighten and become merry. No one was overlooked or forgotten by him; like the young Cratchits, he was 'ubiquitous'. Supper was followed by songs and recitations from the various members of the company, my*

I wish you a right merry Xmas,
I wish you a happy New Year,
I wish I were near you to say so,
To whisper just into your ear,
That tho' absent, thou'rt ever beside me
Tho' parted my soul is with thee
And tho' oceans and seas roll between us,
You can't fancy how dear you're to me.

S.W.

father acting always as master of ceremonies, and calling upon first one child, then another for his or her contribution to the festivity. I can see now the anxious faces turned toward the beaming, laughing eyes of their host. How attentively he would listen, with his head thrown slightly back, and a little to one side, a happy smile on his lips. O, those merry, happy times, never to be forgotten by any of his own children, or by any of their guests. Those merry, happy times!

And in writing thus of these dear old holidays, when we were all so happy in our home, and when my father was with us, let me add this little postscript and greet you on this Christmas of 1892 with my father's own words: 'Reflect upon your present blessings – of which every man has many – not on your past misfortunes, of which all men have some. Fill your glass again with a merry face and contented heart. Our life on it, but your Christmas shall be merry and your New Year a happy one. So may the New Year be a happy one to you, happy to many more whose happiness depends on you! So may each year be happier than the last and not the meanest of our brethren or sisterhood debarred their rightful share in what our great Creator formed them to enjoy.'

The end of Christmas

Twelfth Night is the last day of the Christmas festival and so all of the decorations would be taken down — greenery, Christmas tree, cards and garlands all had to be removed. Failure to do this completely could result in bad luck for the whole of the following year.

When Christmas didn't come

England missed out altogether on Christmas during the time of the Puritans. Regarding the entire business of Christmas as little more than pagan traditions and popish nonsense, they banned it altogether. So from 1652 until 1660, and the restoration of the monarchy, there was no Christmas in England. While the Stuarts, and the kings and queens who followed them, certainly celebrated Christmas, it was not until Victoria's reign that the festivities became the most important time of the year and that it reached such heights of merriment and charity, good cheer and groaning tables. Surely, this was Christmas's finest hour.

Bibliography

Acton, Eliza, *Modern Cookery for Private Families* (London, 1845)

Banffshire Journal, The

Beeton, Mrs, *Book of Household Management* (S. O. Beeton, 1861)

Beeton, Mrs, *Family Cookery* (Ward, Lock & Co, 1899)

Bible, The

Cassell's, *Dictionary of Cookery* (Cassell's, 1874)

Chambers, Robert, *Book of Days* (W. & R. Chambers, 1862-64)

Craig, Diana, *Miscellany of Cook's Wisdom, A* (Running Press, 1992)

Thomas Davies, *Dramatic Miscellanies* (London, 1784)

The Delineator magazine

Dickens, Charles, *Christmas Carol, A* (Chapman & Hall, 1843)

Dickens, Charles, Christmas stories (various) (*Household Words* 1850-62)

Dickens, Charles, *Christmas Tree, A* (*Household Words* 1851)

Dickens, Charles, *Great Expectations* (*All the Year Round*, 1860-61)

Dickens, Charles, *Sketches by Boz* (John Macrone, 1836)

Dickens, Mamie, *My Father as I Recall Him* (*Ladies Home Journal*, 1892)

Evelyn, Right Worshipful Richard, Esq, *Articles* (see Chambers, *Book of Days*)

Francatelli, Charles Elme, *The Cook's Guide and Housekeeper and Butler's Assistant* (Richard Bentley, 1869)

Gaskell, Mrs, *Cranford* (*Household Words* 1853)

Harper's Bazaar (1868, 1873, 1896)

Kilvert, Rev Francis, *Diary of Francis Kilvert, 1870-79* aka *Diary of a Country Curate* (Folio Society, 1977)

Major, L., *The Pytchely Book of Refined Cookery* (Chapman and Hall, 1886)

Moore, Clement Clark, *Night Before Christmas, The* (*The New York Sentinel*, 1823)

Punch magazine (1849)

Rundell, Mrs (Maria), *New System of Domestic Cookery, A* (John Murray, 1805)

Soyer, Alexis, *Shilling Cookery for the People, A* (Routledge & Co, 1855)
Various authors, *Receipt Books*
Walsh, J. H., *The Economical Housekeeper* (Routledge & Co, 1857)
Warne, Mary Jewry, *Model Cookery* (London, 1869)

Permissions

The author would like to thank the following for providing the illustrations in this book:

Lawrences Fine Art Auctioneers of Crewkerne - three bottles (p39)
Shoop, Fiona – Victorian Christmas cards
Thomaston Place Auction Galleries of Thomaston, ME - Victorian toy sleigh (p78) and 1880 doll (p79)

With thanks to Shutterstock for the remainder of the images

Index